WHy T  iTTEN

Why another book on casino blackjack? There are presently over twenty available. Blackjack is undoubtedly the most studied and documented of any of the casino games.

Here are a number of reasons why this book is needed:

- Blackjack books, in general, tend to be too complicated and difficult for the beginner to comprehend. This book is for the beginning to intermediate player and was written from the layman's viewpoint—not the expert's!

- Many of the readers of my column have requested copies of the blackjack series. Since I didn't have the time or resources to accommodate them, this book will accomplish that purpose.

- The number of players is expanding, particularly on the Eastern Seaboard. I want to do my part to ensure that new players are properly introduced to the game.

- The game is changing. The Atlantic City game, in particular, is new to a large number of blackjack players. This book discusses the Atlantic City game in some detail

Also by Jerry L. Patterson

Blackjack: A Winner's Handbook

Blackjack's

Winning Formula

Revised and Expanded Edition

By

Jerry L. Patterson

A Perigee Book

To Nancy with Love—
For being there when I needed her
and helping me make it all happen

Perigee Books are published by
G. P. Putnam's Sons
200 Madison Avenue
New York, New York 10016

Library of Congress Cataloging in Publication Data

Patterson, Jerry L.
    Blackjack's winning formula.

    "A Perigee book."
    Bibliography: p.
    1. Blackjack (Game)   I. Title.
GV1295.B55P38   1982   795.4'2   81-15400
ISBN 0-399-50617-9   AACR2

First Perigee printing, 1982

Printed in the United States of America

Special Acknowledgments

This book is based in part on a series of casino gaming columns I wrote for some very distinguished newspapers. I am proud to be associated with these newspapers and wish to acknowledge them for their decision to publish the column and therefore to help the thousands of casino gamers who need and use the information contained therein. *The Trentonian*: Emil Slaboda; the *Philadelphia Bulletin*: Ed Radamaeker; the *Philadelphia Inquirer* (published weekly for six months): Jay Searcy and Tom Wark; the *Atlantic City Press* (published weekly for two years): Robert Ebener and Charles Wray; the *Courier-Post* (published weekly for one year): Stanley Goldstein and Paul Schwiezer; the *Philadelphia Daily News* (published weekly for two years): Gene Castellano and Debbie Licklider; the *San Francisco Chronicle* (10-part series): Stanleigh Arnold;

the *New York Daily News* (5-part series): John Quinn, Bill
Brink; the *Baltimore Sun* (10-part series): Steven Parks. I
would like to acknowledge Don Schlesinger for proof-
reading and editing this book. Don's helpful suggestions
and constructive comments not only to me but also to
many other blackjack authors have earned him the reputation as the conscience of the blackjack writing com-
munity.

Special note to readers of the first edition

This revised edition contains extensive new material
including four chapters describing my blackjack trips,
practical tips for playing the Las Vegas casinos, and an
update on the war between the Atlantic City casinos and
the card counters, and new and much-needed material
about women blackjack players.

Note to second printing

THE BLACKJACK CLINIC continues to expand. We
have now instructed over 1200 students in blackjack's
winning formula. Classes are offered in New York City,
Philadelphia and New Jersey locations. See Chapter 17 for
details.

Jerry L. Patterson
March 1, 1981

Note to revised and expanded edition

THE BLACKJACK CLINIC now offers classes on a
nationwide basis. We have instructed over 3000 students
in blackjack's winning formula.

Jerry L. Patterson
March 1, 1982

Acknowledgments

Many exciting things have happened to me since I wrote and published my first book, *Blackjack: A Winner's Handbook*, three years ago. The reader response to the book has been overwhelmingly positive. As this new book goes to press, we have sold 12,000 copies of *Blackjack: A Winner's Handbook* and are into the third printing.

The success of this book led to the idea of writing a weekly column on casino games. The Atlantic City casinos were just opening and there was a dearth of information on how to play the games, which bets are best for the player and which bets to avoid. The original idea for the column was Jay Searcy's—the Sports Editor of the *Philadelphia Inquirer*. He helped me and my wife, Nancy, convince Tom Wark—the associate managing editor—to give it a try. I owe both these gentlemen a debt of gratitude.

The column led to a number of appearances on television and radio and helped me generate a reputation as the gambler's advocate in the Philadelphia/South Jersey area. To my knowledge, the column on casino games is the first of its kind.

The dual success of the book and the column motivated me to develop a concept that I had been toying with for quite some time—offering a workshop on blackjack. It seemed to me that there was so much information available on how to beat the game, but too few players were taking advantage of it. I had some ideas for instruction that were totally different from anything that had ever been done before. I offered the Blackjack Workshop to readers of my column in the *Philadelphia Inquirer* who had written to me.

Lo and behold, seven students enrolled and we were under way. I would like to acknowledge and thank these seven players for the confidence they showed in helping me launch what has become a very successful BLACK-JACK CLINIC. I will not mention their names because all of them, to my knowledge, are still playing winning blackjack in the Atlantic City casinos.

Since the Atlantic City casinos opened three years ago, I have played more hands of blackjack than in my prior twenty years of playing the game. It is really a nice feeling to be able to jump in your car and be sitting at a blackjack table less than an hour later.

Anyway, professional blackjack, the management and operation of the BLACKJACK CLINIC and writing have become my full-time occupation. I owe a debt of gratitude to Fred Gross, president of Systems & Computer Technology Corporation (SCT) in Malvern, PA for helping me make this possible. Freddie and I had worked together since 1967 and were both principals in SCT. Freddie approved a very liberal severance pay agreement and arranged for the repurchase of my SCT stock. Without this help I could not have launched my new career.

The success of the BLACKJACK CLINIC has just been incredible. From the original seven, we now instruct about fifty students a month. We have never received a bad student evaluation and a good percentage of our business comes from student referrals. I had considerable help in achieving this success.

I learned a tremendous amount from Kenny Uston. Kenny sort of took Nancy and me under his wing when he was pulling off his $140,000 caper at Resorts in January 1979. We became very good friends and I came to respect Kenny as a world class blackjack player and as a super instructor of blackjack systems methodology.

I am one of the privileged few who know Stanford Wong personally. I respect Wong first of all as a professional blackjack player. Wong plays with impunity in casinos throughout the world and has never had a problem in being barred from play. Wong is creative—an innovator. Wong just doesn't play blackjack; Wong continuously seeks out and develops new winning strategies. I have learned much from Wong's books, newsletters and in the many conversations we have had and wish to acknowledge Wong for this and also for his many important contributions to the game.

There are many others I wish to acknowledge—my instructors and my students for contributing to my own success by becoming successful themselves.

I also wish to acknowledge the Atlantic City casinos for

being there and for providing a very good blackjack game. I regard my relationship with the casinos as one of operating in two different worlds. I am not hurting them and they are not hurting me. The 400 students I have instructed as this book goes to press have made an unnoticeable dent in the casino's bottom line—analogous to a grain of sand on the Atlantic City beaches when compared to the thousands of gamblers who take a shot at their tables on a daily basis. In a sense I have probably added to the casino's bottom line by generating gambling interest as a result of my weekly Casino Gaming Column—it reaches 500,000 homes in this area.

I would like to acknowledge the New Jersey Casino Control Commission for trying to improve the game, but I wish they would stop. The game is just fine the way it is right now. There is no need to change it to the detriment of the general public so a handful of pros can regain the right to play. If the game is changed into one of chance instead of skill, then the pros will have no incentive to play and the general public's interest in the game will fall off. In that way, everybody loses. Because I feel so strongly on this issue, I have dedicated an entire section of this book to it.

Thank you, dear reader, for bearing with me through this somewhat rambling recounting of events and acknowledgments which led to my writing this book.

Jerry L. Patterson

CONTENTS

Section III
Atlantic City Blackjack Rules—
Casinos and Counters Wage an Ongoing War

Section IV
Blackjack in Nevada

SECTION I
Blackjack Basics

Section Overview

In this section you will learn how and why casino blackjack can be beaten by reading a short historical sketch of the game (Chapter 1), learn the fundamentals of how to play the game (Chapter 2), and understand the common myths of blackjack and why they contribute to the poor play of so many players (Chapter 3). *Note:* Readers who do not know how to play the game should first read Chapter 2.

Chapter 1
Blackjack: A Historical Perspective

An Atlantic City casino. Dinner hour—about 6:30 P.M. Throngs of people pouring into the large casino showroom and many casino restaurants. A distinguished-looking man, dressed in a suit and tie, enters the casino, seeks out a $25 minimum blackjack table and sits down to play. There are no other players at the table. The dealer picks up the cards, shuffles the deck and deals. The man bets a green $25 chip. Several hands are played with both sides winning and losing alternately. Suddenly, the player puts four green chips in front of him. He is dealt a 20 to the dealer's 14. The dealer draws an 8 and breaks. The player is paid and leaves the eight chips out for his next hand. He is dealt an 11. The dealer has a 10 showing. Cooly, he bets a second $200 on the hand. For this bet, he is only allowed to draw one more card—he draws a 10 for a perfect hand of 21, beating the dealer's 20. The player picks up his $800 and walks out of the casino—$500 richer. He doesn't even bother to cash in his chips.

We have just seen a blackjack card counter, or "counter" as the casinos refer to them, in action. Employing sophisticated card-counting techniques, the counters are able to determine their exact odds of winning prior to the play of each hand. When the odds favor them, which they do when the deck is rich in 10s or aces, the counters strike. They increase their bet from the minimum allowed to a bet several times as large. They bet high when the deck favors them, low when the deck favors the house. Their long-term advantage varies between 1 and 2%.

Can you duplicate the success of these professional blackjack players? Many have tried. Few have succeeded. Let's see what it's all about. In this book we will distill from their complicated strategies a few simple basics that will be useful for occasional play in Atlantic City, Nevada and the Caribbean.

Now let's look at another card counter, in another Atlantic City casino. He also picks a time when he can play head-to-head against the dealer. The pattern is similar. Chips flow back and forth across the table. The player's stack fluctuates between 15 and 25 green chips. The player is waiting for a hot deck—a deck rich in 10s. He gets it. He bets $100. He draws a 13. The dealer shows a 2. He stands. The dealer flips over a 10 and hits his hand with a breaking 10. More hands are played and our second player is winning consistently. He makes all the right decisions. He doubles down when he is supposed to and splits pairs when it is to his advantage. After thirty minutes of play, he is $1000 ahead.

But now the villain enters: The Pit Boss. His job is to keep an eye on six to eight games and make sure everything is going okay. If there is a dispute, he settles it. He also watches for counters. He has spotted our second player early in his session but he waits for the evidence to build up. He notices the precision play—splitting a pair of 10s against a 6, for example, and pulling a 10 to each split hand.

The verdict is in. He whispers instructions in the dealer's ear. The heat is on. The pit boss is now watching the counter like a hawk. When the counter increases his bet from $100 to $400, to take advantage of favorable odds, the pit moves in for the kill. Flanked by two security guards who read the counter his "rights," he asks him to leave the casino and take his business elsewhere. From this point on the counter will not be welcome in this casino.

You have just witnessed a small battle in a war that started twenty years ago. A war that continues to this day. A war between the casinos and the counters.

In this chapter we will be looking at the tactics and countertactics that are being utilized in this war. We will determine their impact on the occasional or weekend gambler. I will show you how to exploit the strategies being used in this war without becoming a participant. For those who decide to "enlist," the later chapters in the book discuss the pitfalls and what can be done to overcome them.

Some of the strategies are fascinating: Blackjack team play for example that netted one team a bottom line profit of a cool million, or a small personal computer that you wear concealed under your clothes.

But first bear with us for a short historical perspective.

It will give you a greater appreciation of the battles being waged.

Blackjack and computers are the perfect marriage. The courtship began in the late 1950s when four engineers at the Aberdeen Proving Grounds used desk calculators to develop the first basic strategy—a set of rules for hitting, standing, doubling down and splitting pairs. A trial marriage occurred in the early 1960s when Ed Thorp used a high-speed digital computer to prove that black-jack could be beaten by keeping track of the 10s as they are played. Julian Braun of the IBM Corporation con-summated this marriage by playing billions of hands of blackjack on high-speed computers to perfect the basic strategy and Thorp's card-counting techniques.

The reason that computers and blackjack make such good bedfellows is that blackjack rules are well defined and can be easily programmed. A rule for example that says hit 15 if the dealer shows a 9 can be translated to computer code very quickly and easily.

Computers were needed to study the game of blackjack because of the millions of calculations required to deter-mine when to make each blackjack decision and for determining the impact of a shortage or surplus of 10s on the player odds. Three million hands were played, for example, to determine whether or not the player should split a pair of 4s with a 6 showing as the dealer's up-card.

With all this attention on blackjack, the game flour-ished. Thorp's book—*Beat the Dealer*—became a best-seller. Thousands of would-be card counters poured into Las Vegas every weekend looking for easy money. Not understanding basic money management techniques—

how much to bet in proportion to their total bankroll—
they usually went home broke.

There were some big winners who had the powers of
concentration and mental capacity required to use the
complex card-counting formulas in Thorp's book. Bank-
rolled by two well-heeled high rollers, Thorp himself won
tens of thousands of dollars playing in Nevada and
Caribbean casinos. Because of his winnings, Thorp was
eventually barred from play in all Nevada casinos.

Most of the few successful blackjack players of the
1960s were users of Thorp's Ten Count System or the
High-Low Point Count System published in his 1966
version of *Beat the Dealer*. The High-Low System requires
the assignment of a value to each card type: 10s and aces
were given a minus one (− 1) value, 2s, 3s, 4s, 5s and 6s a
plus one (+ 1) value, and 7s, 8s and 9s a value of zero. As
cards were played from the deck, the player kept a mental
cumulative count. For example, if the dealer dealt hands
containing three 10s, an ace, a 5 and a 7, the player
counted minus 3 (three 10s), minus 4 (adjusted for the
ace), minus 3 (adjusted for the 5) and ended the hand
with minus 3 (the 7 counts zero). Because more cards were
dealt that favored the player (10s and aces), the count is
minus and the remaining deck is now unfavorable. If the
count were a plus 3, indicating more low cards dealt and
more high cards remaining in the deck, the odds would
favor the player. The player adjusts his bet depending on
the odds—he bets high when the odds favor him and the
minimum bet when the odds favor the house.

Julian Braun's computer studies produced a plethora of
data that led to the development of a number of advanced

blackjack systems. By the early 1970s, scores of blackjack systems were on the market but, because of their complexity, only a few players were able to exploit them and win big.

A number of blackjack's big winners, now barred from the casinos, turned to system-selling as a way to make a fast buck. They besieged the occasional gambler with promises of quick riches and a life of luxury and travel—by playing winning blackjack in glamorous casinos all over the world.

Books were published as a come-on for the higher-priced system that the author was really touting. High-priced paperbacks were sold in expensive direct mail campaigns. "Blackjack millionaires" appeared on television shows to plug their product. National publications such as the *Wall Street Journal* published lead articles on this extraordinary phenomenon—the game in which the casino could be beaten.

With all this publicity, blackjack soon overtook craps as the most popular casino game. The system sellers made fat profits. But an interesting paradox occurred. The casino's profits increased! As more players learned the game, the casinos added more tables to accommodate this influx. But not only did their profits increase, their rate of profit increased. Their winnings were increasing faster than the number of players.

Why? Because too many occasional gamblers were being taken in by the false promises of the system sellers. It is extremely difficult to apply the data embodied in these complicated card-counting systems. Players were rushing into action too soon and with too small a bankroll to cover their inevitable losing cycles. They didn't realize that the big winners had spent literally hundreds of hours practicing and possessed the self-discipline to become inured to the many distractions of the casino environment. They also had the fat bankrolls necessary to grind out the big profits.

In this book, I will strip the mystique from winning blackjack systems. I will simplify the computer derived formulas into a few simple strategies for the occasional gambler.

Consider the basic playing strategy, for example. This is a strategy for making each blackjack decision: hitting, standing, doubling down, splitting pairs, taking insurance or surrendering. There is a separate decision for each combination of player's hand values. The computer has been programmed to determine the decision with the most favorable odds for each of these 550 combinations. For example, if you are holding a 6, 3 or a total of 9 and the dealer's up-card is a 5, you should double-down. If the dealer's up-card is a 7, you should hit.

Many of the blackjack publications contain complicated tables showing the reader the rules for making each of these 550 decisions. Many hours of practice and an excellent memory are required. I simplified these 550 decision rules to twelve (explained in Chapter 4). It shouldn't take you more than an hour to learn and apply them.

To continue with our historical perspective ... the casinos declared war swiftly after the publication of Thorp's book—*Beat the Dealer*. Thinking that armies of expert card-counters would be invading their heretofore impenetrable fortresses and withdrawing huge sums of money, they changed the rules. They prohibited doubling down on any hand other than 11 and they forbade splitting a pair of aces, which reduced the odds of winning for the basic strategy player.

These actions had the reverse effect. Gamblers simply avoided the game of blackjack. The casino's blackjack profits shrank. The casinos had overreacted. The rule changes were quietly dropped about two weeks later. There were no armies of card counters, simply because Thorp's system was too difficult for the average gambler to use.

The casinos devised other, more subtle, counter-measures. If they suspected a player of counting, they simply shuffled the deck when he made a big bet. This effect was to take away the player's favorable situations. But because shuffling delayed the game and was easily counteracted by the player (he simply raised his bet when the deck was negative to force a return to a neutral deck), the casinos soon discarded this tactic, except to shuffle about three-fourths of the way through the deck to prohibit end-play (knowing the exact values of the remaining cards and betting accordingly).

The casinos soon realized that the counters were much smarter than they were about the underlying mathematics of the game. So they hired their own experts in mathematics and statistics. The casinos then discovered that they could reduce the counters' odds and make it more difficult for them to count by playing the game with more than one deck of cards. The major impact of playing with two, four or six decks is to reduce the number of blackjacks received by the player. This has a greater effect on the player's odds than on the dealer's because the player is paid at 3 to 2 for a blackjack while the dealer only collects even money.

Although this tactic was overcome by the development of point-count systems, today it is difficult to find a casino dealing a one-deck game.* This is because the basic strategy player's odds of winning will be reduced from 0.1% to about −0.5% in the multiple-deck game.

The major weapon employed by the casinos against the counters is barring them from play. If a counter is detected, he is asked to leave the casino and take his business elsewhere. Many of the counters who have been barred are claiming an infringement of their civil liberties. Suits and countersuits have been filed which will probably end up in the Supreme Court.

The successful counters overcome this tactic by exuding the fun-loving attitude of the average gambler. They converse with the other players, ask the dealers stupid questions and get to know the pit bosses. All this while their mind is whirring like a computer to mentally record every card that is played. Their bet variations to take advantage of favorable odds appear totally random to the dealer. Ian Andersen (a pen name) has been using this tactic for about nine years as he describes in his book *Turning the Tables on Las Vegas.* He hides his winnings by surreptitiously removing chips from the table to his coat pocket. He gets others to cash his chips for him or he

---

*A few casinos in Las Vegas offer a small number of one-deck games and all casinos except one or two in Reno/Tahoe offer one-deck games. These are about the only one-deck games in the world.

cashes them in different casinos. The dealers and cocktail waitresses love Ian because he is a lavish tipper. This adds to his image of a high roller and buys him thousands of hours of additional playing time.

The counters use many other tactics. The most famous counter is probably Ken Uston, who led a team of blackjack players to over a million dollars in winnings. Ken's tactic, as documented in his book *The Big Player*, was to deploy each of his counters to a different blackjack table. The counters would make small bets while waiting for a hot deck. When this happened they signaled Ken, who would dash over and plunk down the maximum bet. When the deck cooled, Ken would leave the table and wait for another signal. The pit bosses accepted this errant behavior because Ken looked like a typical high roller who just couldn't wait to get his money down. Once, when two tables got hot simultaneously, he even had the pit bosses placing bets for him.

Ken and his team of counters were not detected for well over a year and not before they had won over a million dollars.

Still another successful tactic is used by Stanford Wong, who makes his living playing blackjack. Spending less than an hour at a time in each casino to avoid overexposure, he pauses at a table where the dealer is shuffling. If the first hand of play produces a positive count, he sits down to play. As soon as the deck turns negative he leaves the table. Because he plays every hand with a positive advantage, he never varies the size of his bet—usually the maximum. This tactic is documented in Wong's book— *Professional Blackjack*.

The ultimate weapon in this war is presently being

"field tested" by a small, elite "special forces" team. It is a small microcomputer concealed under the player's clothing. The player enters the cards played by tapping an input device worn around his leg above the knee. Other sensors, contained in special shoes and positioned to touch the player's feet, signal how much to bet and how to play each hand. The small computer thus relieves the player of the mental burden of card counting. Prototype models of these computers cost about $15,000. From what I have heard they are well worth it, having made their users many thousands of dollars.*

The casinos, of course, are aware of all the tactics described above. Team play such as Uston's has been made very difficult by the Nevada casino practice of "breaking a shoe"—shuffling up anytime a new player enters the game with a large bet (the Atlantic City casinos are prohibited from shuffling up—they must deal two-thirds of a shoe). Other players are watched more closely even with their act of playing the average gambler. The casinos haven't installed any elaborate equipment yet to detect the microcomputers, but if one becomes available for under $500, don't be surprised if, when entering a casino, you are subjected to the same kind of metal detection equipment as you are when entering an airport.

Now what does all of this mean to you—an occasional gambler? Should you learn how to count cards? Is it worth it? How long does it take? Each of these questions will be answered in succeeding chapters in this book. Let's start by defining the basics of the game. Then we will all be working from the same level of knowledge.

---

*Sports Illustrated, April 16, 1979.

CHAPTER 2
How to Play Blackjack

BASIC FUNDAMENTALS

The casino game of blackjack is a card game played between a dealer and from one to seven players. The dealer works for the casino, deals all the hands and handles all the money.

You take a seat at any of the player stations and place your bet (usually from $2 to $500). The dealer deals you two cards, the other players two cards and himself two cards. One of the dealer's cards is exposed and one is unseen. Your objective is to beat the dealer. You can do this in one of two ways: (1) by holding a higher hand than the dealer (i.e., you hold 19, the dealer holds 17) or (2) by not breaking (going over 21, in which case you immediately lose) and waiting for the dealer to break. The dealer always plays his hand last; if he breaks, you win no matter what the value of your hand.

With your initial two cards you determine the value of your hand by simply adding them together. Picture cards count 10 and all other cards count their face value except ace which counts either 1 or 11, whichever is to your advantage. Let's take some examples: A king and a 6 equals 16. An ace and a 7 equal 8 or 18. An ace and a jack is a blackjack or 21. When the first two cards received are an ace and any picture card or 10, the hand is a perfect hand, a "blackjack." If the dealer doesn't have a blackjack too, you win immediately and are paid 1.5 times your bet (i.e., if you're betting $2, you are paid $3).

Casino blackjack involves a precise set of rules for the dealer. The dealer must continue to hit his hand as long as he has 16 or less. He must stand if his hand totals 17 or more. The dealer always plays his hand last. Let's play through a hand to give you an idea of how it all works. You are dealt 5, 3—or 8. With your 8 you now must decide whether to hit (to take another card) or stand (take no more cards). With an 8 (or any hand totaling 11 or less) you would always take another card. Why? Because there is no way you can break (go over 21). You would always improve your hand. Let's say you draw a 10. You now have an 18. Your decision is stand. Why? For one reason, an 18 is not a bad hand. Also, hitting again may break your hand because you are very close to 21.

If you hit your 8 with a 5 for a hand totaling 13, what do you do? You may continue to hit as long as your hand is under 21. The correct hitting or standing decision for this case depends on the dealer's up-card. We will be discussing these "correct" decisions in Chapter 4 when we take up the basic strategy.

Now let's review the objective of the game. Many blackjack books define the objective as getting a hand as close as possible to 21. This is not always true. *The objective is to beat the dealer.* Learning this lesson is your first step on the road to becoming a winning blackjack player. It is possible to beat the dealer by holding a hand that is far less than 21—a 12 or 13 for example.

This is a decision that most beginning players hardly ever make. They think that they must get as close as possible to 21 and thus they hit their hands more than they should. They break more often and contribute to the casino advantage of 6% over the nonsystem player.

The casino rules are defined to give the dealer one major advantage and one major disadvantage. The dealer's advantage is that he always draws last. If you draw cards and break (go over 21), you lose whether the dealer breaks or not.

The dealer's disadvantage is that he must draw as long as he has 16 or less. Therefore, if the dealer has a hand totaling 12 through 16, it is possible that the next card may break him. You, the player, take advantage of this disadvantage by deciding whether to hit (draw another card) or stand (take no more cards).

If the dealer's up-card is 2, 3, 4 or 5, you know he must hit, no matter what the value of his hole card is. Therefore you would stand on a lower hand value, such as 13 and wait for the dealer to break. On the other hand, if the dealer's up-card is a high card, e.g., 9 or 10, you would hit and try to get as close to 21 as possible. This is because there is a good chance that the dealer's hole-card may be another high card. Then his hand would be greater than 16 and he wouldn't have to draw.

After you make your hitting and standing decision, and if you haven't broken, you wait for the dealer to deal to the other players and then to himself. Then your bet is paid if you win, collected if you lose, or left alone if you tie (push).

If your hand contains an ace that is counted as 11 it is known as a "soft" hand. An ace can be counted as either 1 or 11. For example an ace, 6 is a soft 17. An ace, 2 is a soft 13. If you hit an ace, 2 with a 7, you would obviously play the hand as a 20. If you hit the ace, 2 with a 10, the ace now counts as 1 and you play the hand as 13.

All other hands are called "hard" hands. A hard 13 is a 9, 4 or 10, 2, ace, for example.

I have seen inexperienced blackjack players ponder whether to hit or stand for what seemed like several minutes because they had no method for making a decision. They apparently were trying to ordain what the dealer's hole-card was. The dealer and the other players often get upset by this unnecessary delay.

In the Atlantic City casinos, when you make a betting or standing decision, you do it with hand signals.

Pointing at your hand with your index finger or motioning the dealer to "come forward" or "come here" means hit.

ASKING FOR A HIT

A palm-down lateral hand movement over your hand means stand.

STAND SIGNAL

In Atlantic City, never touch your cards. This is against State regulation and prevents cheating by the player and casino.

Also, after making your bet, never touch it until after it is paid. If you wish to double-down or split pairs you move your new bet alongside your original bet.

BLACKJACK DECISIONS

Let's look at four other decisions you can make after you're dealt those first two cards. These decisions are: insurance, double-down, split and surrender.

Insurance

Insurance can be taken when the dealer has an ace showing. You may bet up to half of your original bet that the dealer has blackjack (a picture card or 10 underneath the ace). If he has blackjack, your insurance bet pays 2 to 1. Let's take an example. Your bet is $2 and the dealer shows an ace. You make a $1 insurance bet. If the dealer has blackjack, you lose your $2 bet but you win $2 on your insurance bet, i.e., you break even for the hand. If the dealer does not have blackjack, you lose the $1 insurance bet and continue to play out the hand. Some players take insurance when they have a good hand, e.g., 19, 20 or blackjack. They reason that they have a possible winning hand so why not "insure" it. *Taking insurance is never a good bet unless you are counting cards.*

To understand why insurance is not a good bet when you have a blackjack, consider the following simple example.

Assume: Single-Deck Game with $10 bet
                 □   dealer hole-card
                 A   dealer up-card
                A ⎫
                K ⎭ your hand

Assume: dealer hole-card could be any one of 49 unseen cards.

Now, of the 49 unseen cards, we know that fifteen are 10-value cards (4 tens, 4 jacks, 4 queens, 3 kings). We have one of sixteen 10-value cards—a king—in our hand.

Let's work out the two possibilities:

1. You make a $5 insurance bet
   a. On the average, fifteen times out of 49 (fifteen 10-value cards in 49 unseen cards), the dealer will have blackjack. You win 2 to 1 or $10 on your insurance bet and tie on your blackjack.

$$15 \times \$10 = \$150 \text{ won}$$

b. Thirty-four times out of 49, the dealer will not have blackjack. You lose your insurance bet but are paid 3 to 2 on your blackjack for an effective even money payoff, i.e., you win $15 on your blackjack and lose $5 on your insurance bet for a net win of $10.

$$34 \times \$10 = \$340 \text{ won}$$

Total money won on 49 sample hands = $490

2. You do not make a $5 insurance bet
   a. Fifteen times out of 49, the dealer does have blackjack. You push and win or lose no money.
   b. Thirty-four times out of 49, the dealer will not have blackjack and you are paid off at 3 to 2 or $15 won.

$$34 \times \$15 = \$510 \text{ won}$$

Now, compare the $510 won without taking insurance with the $490 won by taking insurance and you have a $20 higher net win in each 49 hands where this situation occurs.

This same analysis could be done for six decks and the only difference would be a slight reduction in the $20 because of fewer blackjacks in a six-deck game.

Splitting Pairs and Doubling Down

Splitting pairs and doubling down are the two most important decisions in blackjack. This is because the casinos allow you to double your bet on either of these two decisions. To double-down is to double your bet, *but* you are allowed to hit only once—you must take one and only one more card. You make this decision only when it is to your advantage to do so. For example, if you have 11, you should always double-down except against an ace showing. Why? Because there are more 10s in the deck than any other card. A 10 will give you a 21—a perfect hand. Even hitting an 11 with a 7, 8 or 9 will give you a good hand.

Splitting pairs is a situation in which the player is dealt two like cards, e.g., 6, 6. He may split the 6s and play them as two separate hands. If the bet is $2, the player bets an additional $2 on the second 6. As with doubling down, there are advantageous occasions when the player should split the pair. In most cases, these depend on the dealer's up-card.

Remember, when doubling down or splitting pairs, to push your additional bet *alongside* your original bet. Never cap your original bet or the dealer will think you are cheating. Also never touch your original bet.

DOUBLING DOWN

You may push your additional bet out at any time—even before your turn to play.

If you are doubling down, the dealer will arrange your money so that both stacks are inside the circle as in the picture on page 39.

If you are splitting, the dealer will arrange your chips as follows:

This rearrangement is done to show the cameras what the additional money is for. These "eyes in the sky" monitor many of the hands to ensure that no cheating or "skimming" is going on.

Surrender

The surrender decision must be made immediately after being dealt your first two cards. You throw in or surrender your hand. You lose half of your bet. You make this decision when there is a high likelihood of breaking if you hit your hand—on hands totaling 14, 15 or 16 when the dealer most likely has a pat hand (a high card showing) or a potential blackjack. The decision is made to minimize your losses—to salvage half your bet in situations where the dealer will probably beat you.

I call the surrender decision an Atlantic City bonus because surrendering is allowed in only a few Las Vegas casinos. Most casinos do not give the player this extra break. It is also a bonus because you can surrender before the dealer determines whether or not he has a blackjack. At the Atlantic City casinos the dealer does not check his hole-card until after all of the players' hands are finished. Because you can surrender before the dealer checks for a blackjack, Atlantic City surrender is called "early surrender."*

To understand this very favorable rule consider the following hand:

    ☐   dealer hole-card
    A   dealer up-card
    10⎱
      6⎰ your hand with $10 bet

Let's say you surrender, because 16 is the worst possible hand. You lose $5.

Now, all the other players play out their hands. Then the dealer turns over his hole-card—a 10-value card for a blackjack! Even the hands totaling 21 lose their entire bet, e.g., 10, 6, 5. But you've already surrendered and lost only half your bet. A better way of putting it is you've saved half your bet.

A very, very favorable rule indeed. This same hand played in a Las Vegas casino which allows surrender would lose the entire hand. Why? Because the dealer checks for blackjack before any hands are played. If he has it, he turns over the hole-card and scoops up your bet. No surrender!

*Early surrender was eliminated by the New Jersey Casino Control Commission in September 1981.

BLACKJACK JARGON

Blackjack, like other fields of endeavor, tends to take on a language of its own. Below are some of the more common terms.

"stiff"
A bad hand; more specifically, any blackjack hand that could possibly be broken by taking one more card, i.e., 12, 13, 14, 15, 16.

"push"
A tie between player and dealer. No money changes hands.

"anchor"
The anchor position refers to the "third base" seat or the left-most seat as you face the table. Many players mistakenly believe that the anchor person controls the flow of the cards and decides whether to hit or stand in such a way that the dealer gets the breaking card.

"first base"
Opposite from third base, the seat to the far right as you face the table. The first player to make his decisions.

"snapper"
Synonym for blackjack. Not generally used in Atlantic City. If a dealer uses this term, he has probably worked in Nevada.

"toke"   Tip. Money given to the dealer or bet by the player for the dealer.

"soft hand"   Any hand containing an ace where the ace can be counted as 1 or 11, e.g., A,4 is soft 15 and can be played as 5 or 15.

"hole card"   The dealer's unexposed bottom-card.

"cut card"   The yellow or green card given to a player to cut the decks and then inserted by the dealer into the stack to mark the shuffle point.

"burn card"   The first card of the shoe which is unplayed or "burned" and moved right to the discard tray. A new dealer also burns the next card in the shoe.

"counter"   A blackjack player who counts cards and uses this information to determine his advantage.

"basic strategy"   Mathematically and computer derived rules for making each blackjack decision: surrendering, splitting pairs, doubling down, hitting and standing.

CHAPTER 3
Blackjack Myths

Does the "anchor" or third base player affect your chances of winning by how he plays his cards?

Do bad players (players misplaying their hands according to your set of standards) affect your chances of winning? For example, if a player continually splits 10s when he shouldn't, would you leave the table?

Do other players jumping into the game when you are winning affect the "natural order of the cards" and spoil your run of luck?

Do you leave the table if the dealer gets hot?

Does where you sit at the table make a difference in your chances of winning?

Do you seek the "hot table" where the dealer is breaking more often than normal and all the players are winning?

I have been asked the above questions over and over

again by neophyte and experienced blackjack players alike.

The answer to all of these questions is no. This may be hard for you to accept but it is true. The cards fall randomly—not according to a "natural order." Bad play will help you as much as hurt you. In the long run all of the misplayed hands will even out. To confirm this, count the times a misplayed hand at the third base position *helps* you the next time you play. Most players remember only the misplays—they forget about the time the third base player hits a 14 vs. an up-card of 5, pulls a 6, and then the dealer turns over a 10 for a total of 15 and breaks.

It is just incredible how these myths keep perpetuating themselves. Let me tell you some interesting stories.

One night I was playing at Resorts with two other players and all of us were winning consistently. Two young guys walked up to the table, made a single $50 bet, drew a blackjack, and then left. One of the players exclaimed: "That s.o.b. drew my blackjack." They then went on to lose their next few bets and blamed it all on disturbing the natural order of the cards.

I have been lectured to by dealers and players alike about this extraordinary phenomenon: the natural order of the cards. I was playing at the Resorts Casino one night when a dealer and a player began instructing me in how to observe the natural order of the cards. Since part of my cover is to play along with all these myths, I listened intently. "It all started with Thorp," the player informed me. "He wrote a book on card counting. When there are more 10s left in the deck you have a better chance of winning if you know enough not to take the dealer's 10.

Also, the whole theory of card counting is based on the natural order of the cards."

I asked how I would know if that next card is to be a 10. "You have to watch the table," he said. "Get a feel for the order of the cards. And know how many 10s are left to be played."

All the while the deck was getting rich in 10s—and my bet was increasing accordingly. At this time two additional players walked up to our table and played a hand. The player on my right surrendered an 18 to a 10—a ridiculous play. The dealer turned over a blackjack and everybody lost.

"Now that's what I mean. Those two guys came up and disturbed the natural order of the cards," my informant asserted, the dealer shaking his head in agreement. "That's why I surrendered," the guy on my right chimed in.

Have you ever had some well-intentioned player play his own hand in deference to yours? It's happened to me.

Playing at a $5 table and betting $75, I was dealt an A,6 against a dealer up-card of 5. I pushed out my $75 to double-down. The player on my right, sitting in first base and betting $5, asked me whether I wanted him to hit or not. He had a 12. He said he would play the hand the way I wanted because I had the big bet out. I told him politely that it didn't really matter and that he should do what he wanted to do. He said that he would normally stand on the hand but for me he would take a hit. He hit and broke. I doubled and pulled a 4 for a perfect 21. I thanked him very much for his "insight."

Space limitation prohibits my telling you a hundred other stories about the blackjack myths. The best way to handle these myths is first of all to accept them as just that.

Remember that the cards fall randomly. And when someone takes your card, the next one out of the same shoe may be even better. If the dealer tells you that she has been hot, go ahead and sit down and play anyway. The cards have no memory!

Secondly, have some fun with the blackjack myths. Compliment the third base player when he makes the right decision and the dealer breaks. Frown and complain when someone disturbs the "natural order" of the cards. Go along with the other players when they accept these myths.

But never, never let them affect your play!

SECTION II

Blackjack's Winning Formula—The Atlantic City Game

Section Overview

In this section, you will learn blackjack's four-part winning formula:

Part I: The Basic Strategy (Chapter 4)
Part II: Card Counting (Chapter 5)
Part III: Money Management (Chapter 6)
Part IV: Casino Comportment (Chapter 7)

Although this section is mainly concerned with the Atlantic City rules, the theory, axioms and principles discussed relate to any blackjack game.

Chapter 4
The Basic Strategy

INTRODUCTION

Casino blackjack has been studied more thoroughly than any other game of chance. This is because the rules of blackjack are easily expressed by mathematical formulas on high-speed computers. Over nine billion hands of blackjack have been played on computers since Professor Edward O. Thorp discovered the mathematical solution to the game in the early 1960s. The basic playing strategy is the most important result of this extensive computer research. This strategy yields the best or most profitable decisions for making all of the blackjack decisions: hitting, standing, taking insurance, doubling down, splitting pairs and surrendering.

To understand the basic strategy you should remember there are three variables involved in making a blackjack decision: your two cards and the dealer's up-card. Suppose that your hand contains a 6, 3—a value of 9. The dealer's up-card could be one of 10 possibilities: A, 2, 3, 4 . . . 10. Now your best decision if the dealer shows a 3 is to double-down. If the dealer shows a 7, you would hit. There are 550 combinations of player's two cards and dealer's up-card. Therefore there are 550 different blackjack decisions. Fortunately many of these decisions are similar. They can be learned as twenty-three rules.

Obviously, following these decision rules, you cannot win every hand. But in the long run the basic strategy yields the best chance for making a profit. In the six-deck Atlantic City game, your average long-term disadvantage is 0.4%.* In the next chapter, when you learn the card-counting techniques, your chances of winning will increase.

Let's take an example of the twenty-three basic strategy rules. If you're dealt a 15, you stand if the dealer's up-card is 2, 3, 4, 5, 6. You hit if the up-card is 7, 8 or 9. You surrender if the up-card is a 10 or ace. If your 15 is comprised of more than two cards, you change the surrender rule to hit because you're only allowed to surrender your first two cards. For example, if you are dealt a 5, 3 and then hit and receive a 7, you hit again if a 10 or ace shows. The reason behind standing if a 2-6 shows is that the dealer must hit his hand no matter what card he has underneath (with one exception—an ace

---

*When early surrender was in effect, the player had a 0.2% advantage.

underneath a 6). Your chances of winning are better if you don't take the chance of breaking. For example, with your 15, you could break if you hit with a 7, 8, 9 or 10. Since there are 28 cards that could break you, why take the chance? If you break, you lose no matter what the dealer does. Wait and let the dealer take the chance. He must hit his hand as long as it's 16 or less. He has no choice.

That should give you an idea of how the basic strategy works. Now let's discuss the basic strategy for each decision in detail. Then we will tabulate the full basic strategy table.

DOUBLING DOWN—HARD HANDS

Doubling down, one of the more important decisions covered by the basic strategy, means doubling your bet after the first two cards are dealt but only being allowed to draw one more card.

The Atlantic City rules allow you to double-down on any two cards except a blackjack. In this section we will discuss the rules for doubling down on player hands totaling 9, 10 or 11 for the six-deck game.

The basic strategy rules for these hands are:

1. If your hand totals 11 (e.g., 6-5), double-down unless the dealer's up-card is an ace.
2. If your hand totals 10 (e.g., 7-3), double-down when the dealer's up-card is 2 through 9.
3. If your hand totals 9 (e.g., 5-4), double-down when the dealer's up-card is 3 through 6.

The reasons for these rules are fairly obvious. Since there are more 10s in the deck than any other card, you have a good chance of drawing a 10 to a doubling-down hand. A 10 drawn to an 11 yields a 21—an unbeatable hand (except against a dealer blackjack).

A 10 drawn to a 10 yields a 20, enough to beat the dealer's hand in all but one case—if his hole-card is an ace (unless, of course, the dealer must hit his hand, but then the odds are even better that you will beat him).

The player holds sizable advantages in these doubling-down situations as explained in the following table:

Hand	Player Advantage	Profit per 100 bets of $2 each
9	2%	$ 4
10	24%	$48
11	40%	$80

DOUBLING DOWN ON SOFT HANDS

Many beginning blackjack players are prone to make mistakes with soft hands. A soft hand is any hand containing an ace where the ace is counted as 11 or 1. For example, an ace, 4 can be played as either a 5 or a 15. I have seen many players draw an ace, 4—(soft 15), look at it for a long few seconds and, not knowing what to do, stand. There is no way that you can hurt a soft 15. If you hit it with a 10, the ace will count as 1, and you have a hard 15. In other words, there is no way you can break, so you might as well take another card. If you draw a 3, 4, 5 or 6 you have a standing hand. Even if you draw a 10, you are no worse off, you still have a 15.

It is to your advantage to double-down on certain hands. Before we discuss these let's look at the soft hands for which you do not double-down.

A,A   (soft 12)
A,8   (soft 19)
A,9   (soft 20)
A,10   (blackjack)

Two aces are always split and played as 11. You have a much better chance of winning by splitting the aces.

Soft 19 and 20 are standing hands. In most cases you will beat the dealer.

An ace, 10 is, of course, the "name of the game," or blackjack, and you win $3 for every $2 you bet on this hand.

The soft hands that you do double-down on if the dealer shows the corresponding up-card are as follows:

Soft Hand	Dealer's Up-card
A,2 (13)	5,6
A,3 (14)	5,6
A,4 (15)	4,5,6
A,5 (16)	4,5,6
A,6 (17)	3,4,5,6
A,7 (18)	3,4,5,6

You are obviously doubling down when the dealer has the best chance of breaking. Therefore, there are two ways you can win. Let's use soft 16 as an example. You could draw an ace through a 5 to end up with a standing total of 17 through 21. Your standing hand could either tie or beat the dealer's hand. If you draw a 6 through a 10, you haven't helped your hand but you still win if the dealer breaks.

This strategy doesn't always work but it will win more money for you in the long run. For example, if you hit an A,5 vs. a dealer 6 you will win, on the average, 12 cents out of each dollar bet. But if you double-down instead you will win 22 cents out of each dollar bet—a large gain of 10 cents.

When I first started playing the basic strategy in the late 1950s, the dealers were amazed when I doubled-down on a soft hand. They thought it was a very stupid play and would attempt to advise me against it. I would just smile and insist on making the bet. They thought it was only luck when I beat them.

Over the years, the dealers have become familiar with the basic strategy and now recognize the soft double as the intelligent bet that it is.

When you spot a player making this bet, you will know that he is playing the basic strategy.

SPLITTING PAIRS

You can increase your gain by knowing when to split pairs. Splitting pairs is a situation in which you are dealt two like cards, e.g., 6,6. You split the 6s and play them as two separate hands. If the bet is $2, then you bet an additional $2 on the second six.

The basic strategy rules for splitting pairs in the Atlantic City six-deck game are shown below.

	Splitting Rule
Pair	**Dealer's Up-card**
A-A	Always
5-5 or 10-10	Never
2-2; 3-3; 7-7	2,3,4,5,6 or 7
4-4	5 or 6
6-6	2,3,4,5 or 6
8-8	2,3,4,5,6,7,8 or 9
9-9	2,3,4,5,6,8 or 9
	(stand on 7)

Aces should always be split because each ace counts as 11—draw a 10 to either ace and you have a perfect hand of 21. (Not a blackjack in this case—a blackjack is an ace, 10 on the first two cards only.) When splitting aces you are allowed to draw only *one* card to each ace. In other pair-splitting situations you may draw as many cards as you like.

Since a hand totaling 16 is about the worst possible, two 8s should always be split except when a 10 or ace shows, then surrender. You don't necessarily increase your profits by splitting 8s—you decrease your losses.

Splitting two 8s against a 7 is the most important play in blackjack. If you play the two 8s as a 16 and hit them, you will lose about 37 cents of each dollar bet on this situation. If you split the two 8s against the 7 you will win about 26 cents out of each dollar bet on this situation—a gain of 63 cents (37 + 26).

Tens should never be split for obvious reasons—why break up a winning hand? It is to your advantage to play a pair of 5s as a 10 and double-down if the dealer shows a 2 through a 9. A pair of 5s should never be split, simply because it will cost you money to do so.

The basic strategy rules for splitting 2s, 3s, 4s, 6s, 7s and 9s have been worked out through the use of probability theory and computer studies. Memorize these rules with the confidence that they are 100 percent accurate—using them reduces the casino advantage to an absolute minimum.

Adding a small percentage to the player's advantage are the Atlantic City rules which allow you to double-down after splitting pairs. If you split a pair of 6s, for example, and hit the first 6 with a 5, you can double-down on this split hand. This decision is discussed in the next section.

Subtracting a small percentage from your advantage is the rule which prohibits you from resplitting a third like-card—a third 3 dealt to a split 3, for example.

DOUBLING DOWN
AFTER SPLITTING PAIRS

The New Jersey Casino Control Commission adopted two liberal blackjack rules to partially balance the advantage the casinos derive from the six-deck game. In Nevada, the casinos hold a ½% advantage in a four-deck game against a basic strategy player who doesn't count cards. In a one-deck game, this advantage is nullified.

But, at the Atlantic City casinos, take advantage of the following two liberal rules and play the basic strategy as described in this book and you will gain a small advantage—you win about 20 cents out of each 100 dollars bet (a 0.2% advantage):

1. You may double-down after splitting pairs.
2. You may surrender your hand after being dealt the first two cards and lose half your bet.*

The first rule is the topic of this section. Betting $5, suppose you are dealt two 6s with the dealer showing a 5. Naturally you split them, put another $5 on the second 6 and play them as two separate hands. Suppose you draw a 5 to your first 6. You may double-down on this new hand by adding another $5 to the $5 bet on this hand and drawing only one more card. You now have a total of $15 bet instead of just $5. In addition, the odds are working for you because the dealer figures to break. Let's say you draw a 10 to your 6,5. So far, so good. Now the best the dealer can hope for is to tie you.

The dealer now deals to your second 6—a 10. Playing the dealer to break, you stand on this 16. The dealer draws a 10 and breaks. You collect $15 instead of $5. These are the types of plays that eliminate the house advantage of 6% over the nonsystem player and provide the basic strategy player with a positive advantage of 0.2%. The above sequence looks like this:

---

*This rule was eliminated in September 1981, but this discussion is left intact because the rule may be restored. The player's basic strategy disadvantage without surrender is 0.4%.

TWO 6s DEALT.

TWO 6s SPLIT;
BET DOUBLED TO $10.

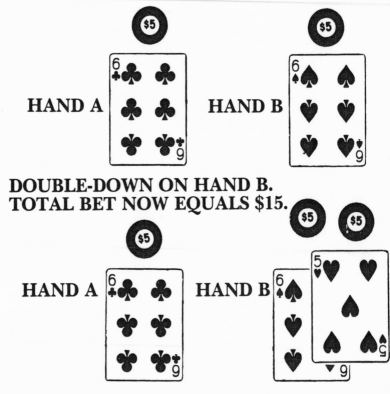

HAND A   **HAND B**

DOUBLE-DOWN ON HAND B.
TOTAL BET NOW EQUALS $15.

HAND A   **HAND B**

FINAL HANDS DRAWN
FROM SPLIT 6s.

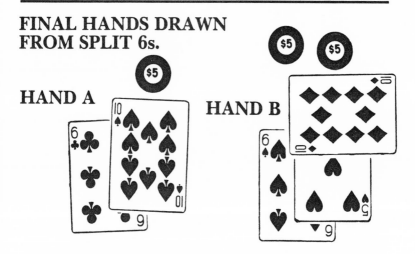

Few beginning blackjack players split pairs when it is to their advantage to do so. Fewer still know when to double-down after splitting. On one occasion, I was playing next to a gentleman who had luck running with him. He was pulling 19s and 20s when the dealer was drawing 18s and 19s. Betting $25 chips, he won a quick $500. Over the next few hands, he received a number of double-down and pair-split opportunities. He drew an 11, did not double-down, and hit it with a 10. He held a soft 15 against a dealer up-card of 6 and did not double-down. He hit this hand with a 5. He failed to split a pair of 7s against a 4. At my urging, he finally split a pair of 8s against an up-card of 6. When he pulled a 3 on the first 8, I couldn't talk him into doubling down. You guessed it— he drew a 10. This gentleman walked away ahead about $1000. Playing basic strategy he could have won between $1500 and $2000.

THE SURRENDER DECISION

The Early Surrender basic strategy for Atlantic City blackjack was derived in September 1978 by Julian Braun and, independently, by Stanford Wong.

Because the dealer does not check his hole-card until after all the hands have been played, it is possible for you to surrender against a blackjack. Therefore, when the dealer has an ace or a 10 showing, you will surrender all of your bad hands.

Against an ace you surrender all two-card totals of 5,6,7,12,13,14,15,16,17 including the pairs: 3-3, 6-6, 7-7, 8-8 (you are allowed to surrender only on your first two cards). All of these hands are low-percentage hands with a high probability of breaking, so the idea is to get rid of them and save half your bet. If your two-card hand contains an ace, you do not surrender, because a soft hand is never a bad hand—you always get two chances to improve it.

Against a 10 you surrender all hard totals of 14,15,16 including the pairs: 7-7, 8-8. You do not surrender as many hands against a 10 because the dealer has less chance of having a blackjack.

Against a 9 you surrender a 16 if your 16 is 10,6 or 9,7. If your 16 is 8-8, you split the 8s and do not surrender. On this latter hand, you are playing the percentages. 8-8 vs. 9 is a losing hand but you lose *less* by splitting than by surrendering.

THE FULL BASIC STRATEGY

The basic strategy for Atlantic City blackjack is tabulated in Table A. The rules of each hand as a function of the dealer's up-card are given.

The basic strategy in these tables works for both a four-deck and six-deck game. At the present time there are only a few four-deck games, but I expect this to change as more casinos open and competition increases.

SIMPLIFIED BASIC STRATEGY FOR ATLANTIC CITY BLACKJACK

Those readers playing occasional blackjack (once or twice a month) and not wanting to take the time to learn the full basic strategy should learn the following rules. In the interest of simplification, these rules are not totally consistent with the full basic strategy.

1. Always:
    • Stand on hard 17 or higher
    • Stand on soft 18 or higher
    • Hit 8 or lower
    • Double down on 11
    • Split a pair of aces or 8s

2. Never:
    • Split 10s or 5s
    • Take insurance

3. If the Dealer Shows 2,3,4,5 or 6 (low cards):
   - Never hit a breaking hand (a hard hand totaling 12,13,14,15 or 16)
   - Split any pair except 10s or 5s
   - Double-down on 9,10 or 11 on your first two cards or after pair splits
   - Double-down on soft 13 through soft 17

4. If the Dealer Shows an Ace, 10 or Face Card:
   - Stand on hard 17 or soft 19 or above
   - Hit all other hands until you get hard 17 or soft 19 or better

5. If the Dealer Shows 7, 8 or 9:
   - Stand on hard 17 or soft 18 or above
   - Hit all other hands until you get hard 17 or soft 18 or better

Table A
Basic Strategy Rules for the Atlantic City Four-deck and Six-deck Games

Player's Hand	Rules for Dealer's Up-Cards
5–7	Surrender on ace. Otherwise hit.*
8	Always hit.
9	Double on 3-6. Otherwise hit.
10	Double on 2-9. Hit on 10,A.
11	Double on 2-10. Hit on A.
12	Stand on 4-6. Surrender on A. Otherwise hit.*
13	Stand on 2-6. Surrender on A. Otherwise hit.*

14	Stand on 2-6. Surrender on 10,A. Otherwise hit.*
15	Stand on 2-6. Surrender on 10,A. Otherwise hit.*
16	Stand on 2-6. Surrender on 10,A. Surrender (10,6 or 9,7) on 9. Otherwise hit.*
17	Surrender on A. Otherwise stand.†
18-21	Always stand.
A,2	Double on 5,6. Otherwise hit.
A,3	Double on 5,6. Otherwise hit.
A,4	Double on 4-6. Otherwise hit.
A,5	Double on 4-6. Otherwise hit.
A,6	Double on 3-6. Otherwise hit.
A,7	Double on 3-6. Stand on 2, 7, 8. Hit on 9, 10, A.
A,8-A,10	Always stand.
A,A	Always split.
2,2	Split on 2-7. Otherwise hit.
3,3	Split on 2-7. Surrender on A. Otherwise hit.*
4,4	Split on 5,6. Otherwise hit.
5,5	Never split. Treat as 10 above.
6,6	Split on 2-6. Surrender on A. Otherwise hit.*
7,7	Split on 2-7. Surrender on 10, A. Otherwise hit.*
8,8	Surrender on 10,A. Otherwise split.‡
9,9	Split on 2-6, 8, 9. Stand on 7, 10, A.
10,10	Always stand.

* Without surrender, always hit.
† Without surrender, always stand.
‡ Without surrender, always split.

Basic Strategy Axiom

To derive the 0.2% player advantage with surrender or the 0.4% minimal house advantage without surrender, you must play basic strategy the same way every time. Do not vary your decisions and do not play hunches. You will not win every hand but you will win more and lose less in the long run.

QUESTIONS AND ANSWERS

The questions posed below are real ones submitted by readers of my weekly newspaper column on casino gaming. They will serve to amplify the prior discussion on the basic strategy.

Question (J.C.): Does the surrender decision have a 22½% house advantage? Answer: Definitely not so. Properly played, surrender gives the player an advantage of 0.6%. This 22½% figure is an error that was first published in John Scarne's book—*Scarne's Guide to Casino Gambling* (p. 46).

Question (H.H.): Do the surrender rules (as discussed in this chapter), apply to one-, two-, or four-deck games and do they permit surrendering in Las Vegas? Answer: The surrender rules are good for one-, two-, four- and six-deck games. The surrender rules are good only for

Atlantic City because of "early surrender"—you are allowed to surrender before the dealer determines whether or not he has a blackjack. Only a few Las Vegas casinos permit surrendering: Caesars Palace, Dunes, Riviera, Desert Inn, El Cortez and the Las Vegas Club. A different surrender strategy should be played in these casinos because you cannot surrender if the dealer has a blackjack (see Chapter 11).

Question (T.C.): If the dealer's first two cards are an ace, 4 (5 or 15) and he hits with a 2 (dealer's hand is now soft 17), does the dealer hit or stand? Answer: The dealer must stand on all 17s including soft 17s (containing an ace counting as 11).

Question (P.D.): When do I insure against a blackjack? Answer: Never take insurance—not even with blackjack. The casino pushes insurance, especially on a blackjack, because of the high house percentage—about 8%. It is true that when you insure a blackjack, you cannot lose (you either win 2 to 1 on your insurance bet if the dealer has the blackjack or 3 to 2 on your blackjack if the dealer doesn't have the blackjack), but you are in effect giving up the 50% bonus paid on the blackjack. Let's say you're betting $10. You put up $5 for the insurance bet for a total of $15 wagered on the hand. If the dealer has the blackjack, your original $10 is "pushed" (you do not lose it) and you win $10 on the insurance bet. If the dealer does not have the blackjack, you lose the insurance bet, but are paid $15 for the blackjack. Either way you win $10. But without taking insurance you win $15. In the long run you're better off not taking insurance.

Question (M.L.): What do I do if the player has a 17

and the dealer shows an 8? Answer: If your 17 is a hard hand, you always stand (except surrender against an ace). If your 17 is soft, you always hit.

Question (E.G.): What do I do when holding a face card and deuce against a dealer up-card of 2 when playing third base (the leftmost seat as you face the table)? Answer: Hit on any hand totaling 12 against a dealer up-card of 2.

Question (E.M.): Does the seating arrangement give anyone an advantage? Answer: First of all, where you sit has absolutely no effect on your decision. Your decision depends on your two cards and the dealer's up-card. It is a myth that the third-base player can control the fall of the cards and have an effect on whether or not the dealer breaks. The cards fall randomly. Play your hand for yourself and not for the potential benefit of the other players.

Question (F.M.): Is the dealer allowed any mistakes such as dealing a card accidentally or forgetting to bury the card? Answer: A card drawn in error is covered very clearly in the Commission regulations—". . . shall be dealt to the players or dealer as though it were the next card from the shoe. Any player refusing to accept such card shall not have any additional cards dealt to him during such round." Sometimes you can take advantage of this rule by seeing an exposed card that the player sitting to your right doesn't want. Recently I was prepared to hit a hand totaling 15 against a dealer up-card of 8 when the player on my right refused to accept a 6 and surrendered his hand. Think about what you would do in this situation knowing the 6 is your next card. The answer is double-down—you cannot lose.

Other irregularities are not so well covered by the regulations. Normally, a dealer forgetting to bury a card or forgetting to deal himself (I have seen this happen) will take the next card in the shoe. The cards will not be backed up to make up for these types of errors.

Question: A number of readers have asked about the early surrender decision. Answer: This decision has the largest effect on your chances of winning—a contribution of 0.6% (without early surrender your chances of winning would be −0.4%, not +0.2%). The reason is as follows. Assume you are betting $10 and surrender your hand to an ace up-card—you lose $5 and save $5. The dealer plays out all the hands and then turns over a blackjack. You have only lost half your bet to a blackjack. In Nevada, on the same hand, you lose $10. This is because the dealer checks his hole-card *before* the hands are played. If he has a blackjack, he turns it right over and collects your $10.

Question (G.L., J.L.): What about the strategy of never hitting a breaking hand, that is, never hitting a 12 or higher, but sticking with the idea that you're "in" every hand and the dealer may break? Answer: Following this strategy is a mistake that many blackjack players make. The correct play is to hit a 12,13,14,15 and 16 if the dealer shows a 7,8,9; surrender each of these hands against an ace; surrender the 14-16 against a 10; and surrender a 16 (10,6 or 9,7) against a 9.

Hands totaling 12 to 16 are not moneymakers because they are the worst possible hands you can get. The player that hits or surrenders these hands will lose less money in the long run. The reason you hit is that the dealer either has a standing hand (17-21) or has a good chance of drawing a standing hand. You have to hit your hand in an attempt to beat him.

Question (T.M.): Does the introduction of six decks of cards at the blackjack tables increase the casino's advantage? Answer: If you are just playing basic strategy (making the correct surrendering, splitting, doubling, hitting and standing decisions), then the answer is a qualified yes—the casino's advantage is increased only slightly—about 0.05%. The player following basic strategy rules enjoys a tiny advantage of about 0.22% in a four-deck game. This advantage decreases to about 0.17% in a six-deck game.

If you are counting cards the answer is yes—the casino's advantage is affected. The player has the advantage in card counting and this advantage is reduced slightly in a six-deck game. I will discuss this at some length in Chapter 5.

Question (V.S.): Should one's decision as to whether to hit or stand be based in any way on the cards that the other players have showing and on the number of players in the game? Answer: First of all, your decision should not be based on the number of players in the game. Secondly, unless you are counting cards and can use this information to vary the basic strategy, you should not base your decision on the cards the other players have showing. It is better to stick to the basic strategy.

Question (C.B.): Why do you hit soft 18 (A-7) when

dealer shows 9, 10 or ace? Answer: 18 is just not that good a hand. You have to assume the dealer has a 19 or 20 and has you beaten. Therefore, you must draw to attempt to beat him. If the casino offered you an 18 on every hand with the dealer following universal rules (hitting 16 or less, standing on 17 or more), would you take this bet? It sounds good, doesn't it? But you would lose over half the time with your 18. So don't put that much confidence in your soft 18 when the dealer shows a 9, 10 or ace. Go ahead and hit it until you get hard 17 or soft 19 or better.

Question (C.B.): The Atlantic City Basic Strategy says split 2s, 3s, 7s on dealer up-cards of 2-7. Other basic strategies indicate splitting these hands on 4-7. Why the difference? Answer: You split more often in Atlantic City because you are allowed to double-down after splitting. It is possible that, starting with a $5 bet, you could split, double-down on each split hand and work your bet up to $20. This rule contributes 0.1% to your overall basic strategy advantage of 0.2%.

Question (M.R.): In basic strategy, is doubling down on an 8 a good bet if the dealer's up-card is a 4, 5 or 6? Answer: No. If your 8 consists of two 4s, then you would split on an up-card of 5 or 6. Other 8s (5,3, or 6,2) should be hit on a 4, 5 or 6.

Question (M.R.): Should you double-down on a 10 or 11 if the dealer shows a 10- or ace-up? If the dealer has a blackjack, he returns your double-down bet so wouldn't this bet enhance basic strategy? Answer: You should double-down only on 11 vs. 10-up. The other double-downs are just not percentage plays. You could still lose both bets if the dealer does not have blackjack. Remember that the ace is the most powerful card because it is played as a 1 or 11. The dealer has a better chance to make his hand than you do by just drawing one more card on the double. If you double on 10 vs. 10-up, you may be doubling against a 20, which is a tough hand to beat.

Chapter 5
How to Win by Counting Cards

WHY CARD COUNTING WORKS

Before you learn to win at blackjack you should understand why it can be beaten. The theory of winning blackjack involves card counting. Your probability of winning is dependent upon those cards remaining to be played. Therefore, if you keep track of the cards as they are played, you know what your chances are of winning the next hand. If your chances are better than even, raise your bet. If the odds are less than even, make a minimum bet. You do not count all the cards—only those that most directly affect your probability of winning. These are 10s, aces and fives. The odds are in your favor when the deck is rich in 10s and aces and short in 5s. A normal deck has sixteen 10s (four 10s, four jacks, four queens, four kings) and 36 others for a total of 52 cards. For an example of a deck rich in 10s, assume that twelve cards have been dealt—all non-10s. The remaining deck now contains sixteen 10s and 24 others. Computer studies have shown that any time the ratio of non-10s to 10s is less than two, the odds are in your favor. In this case, the ratio is $^{24}/_{16}$ or 1.5, so you should make a big bet.

It is obvious why the deck is in your favor when it is rich in 10s and aces; you will be dealt more blackjacks and more standing hands (17, 18, 19, 20). The dealer will also receive an equal share of these better hands, but the dealer does not get paid 3-2 on a blackjack; the dealer cannot double-down on a 9, 10 or 11 with a better chance of receiving a 10; the dealer cannot split a pair when the odds are in his favor; the dealer must always hit stiffs (12-16) with a better chance of breaking.

A surplus of 5s increases the dealer's probability of winning because a 5 will turn any stiff (12-16) into a standing hand (17-21). Therefore, the fewer 5s there are in the deck, the less the dealer's chances of winning.

To prove that card counting works, remove the 5s and 6s from the deck and then deal practice hands from this partial deck. On the average, you will win money in seven out of ten sessions (100 hands per session).

THE HIGH-LOW SYSTEM

"High-Low," a simple point-count system, will enable you to determine easily whether or not the deck is rich in

10s and aces. It was developed in 1963 by Harvey Dubner and was initially published in the second edition of Ed Thorp's *Beat the Dealer*. It has been refined over the years by Julian Braun and Stanford Wong through the play of billions of hands on high-speed computers and was published in Stanford Wong's *Professional Blackjack* and Julian Braun's *How to Play Winning Blackjack*.

High-Low is played as follows:

2,3,4,5,6	(low cards)	count as $+1$
7,8,9	(neutral cards)	count as 0
10,J,Q,K,A	(high cards)	count as -1

You simply start with zero for a freshly shuffled deck or shoe and count each card that you see. For example, if the following cards are played: 2,4,5,10,7,8,6,4,5,5—you would count as follows $+1$ (the 2 counts as $+1$), $+2$ (the 4), $+3$ (the 5), $+2$ (the 10 counts as -1), $+1$ (the J), $+1$ (the 7 counts as zero), $+1$ (the 8), $+2$ (the 6), $+3$ (the 4), $+4$ (the 5), $+5$ (the 5).

When your count is plus you generally have a favorable deck because more low cards have been played; more high cards remain in the deck. Conversely, if the count is minus, more 10s, face cards and aces have been played and the advantage is in favor of the casino.

The count has two purposes: (1) to vary the bet size and (2) to vary the basic strategy.

Varying the basic strategy is an advanced blackjack technique and will not be taken up in this book. Varying the bet size is inherent to winning blackjack. When the count increases, your chance of winning increases. The higher your chances of winning, the more you should bet. We will discuss this at length in the next chapter.

HOW TO COUNT IN THE CASINO

It takes practice to become a skilled card counter. I require the students in my BLACKJACK CLINIC to practice at least an hour a day over the four-week duration of the course and two to three hours a week thereafter. They work with seven card-counting drills to perfect their skills. If you are interested in learning these drills, refer to Chapter 17 and contact me for information about the BLACKJACK CLINIC. An example is described below.

Sample Drill

Try counting down a deck of cards by turning over one card at a time and keeping a "running count." At the end of the deck, your count should be zero, because the twenty high cards cancel out the twenty low cards, and the twelve neutral cards count zero.

Card-Counting Axiom

The only way to win consistently at black-jack is by counting cards. Betting progressively against wins or losses is gambling: if you are lucky, you win; if you are unlucky, you lose. Card counting is percentage playing; you grind out the casino like they grind out all the losing gamblers.

QUESTIONS AND ANSWERS

Question (P.J.O.): I don't believe you can win by counting cards. Is there a way to win by playing only basic strategy? Answer: First of all, you can win at blackjack by counting cards. Blackjack is different from the other casino games in that your odds of winning any given hand depend on the cards remaining to be played. In roulette each spin of the wheel is an independent event and does not depend on what happened in the past. If red comes up thirteen times in a row, the chances that red will come up on the next spin are still the same. In blackjack your odds of winning, to a large extent, are dependent on the 10s and aces remaining to be played. If the remaining deck is rich in 10s and aces, your chances of winning increase. For example, in a one-deck game, if twelve cards are dealt—all non-10s—the remaining deck still contains the original sixteen 10s (four 10s, four jacks, four queens, four kings). One reason your chances of winning increase is because you have a better chance of getting a blackjack with a 3 to 2 payoff (the dealer collects only your original bet if he gets a blackjack—he gets no bonus).

The basic strategy for Atlantic City as published herein yields a small player-advantage of 0.2%. This advantage, however, occurs in the long run—over thousands of hands. In any one session or even over a series of sessions, you could win or lose—big or small, depending on how much you're betting. My advice to all readers of this book is to play the basic strategy without second-guessing or playing hunches. You will not win every time, but you're much better off in the long run. After all, where else can you find an even game?

Question (E.E.): Is there a simple way to count cards quickly? Answer: Yes. Use the High-Low System as discussed earlier in this chapter. To review: low cards (2,3,4,5,6) count +1; neutral cards (7,8,9) count zero; high cards (10,J,Q,K,A) count −1. Start with zero after the shuffle and count every card that you see. Practice at home by counting down a deck of cards—one card at a time. At the end of the deck, your count should be zero.

Question (S.K.): Doesn't the fact that they always shuffle the deck before the end of the shoe and more than one deck is used at a time render the High-Low Counting system useless? Answer: No. The High-Low Count (the running count) is the indicator of the player's advantage. The higher the count, the better your chances of winning the next hand. But remember—you are not guaranteed the winning of the next hand. You will win more often and win more money than you lose. When the count is high you should increase your bet.

Although the shuffle point has no effect on your advantage for the next hand, it does reduce your overall advantage. You are better off being dealt four decks out of a six-deck shoe than three decks. This is because you have more chances for a favorable situation (high count). In Atlantic City, the regulations stipulate that the casinos deal at least four decks before reshuffling. (The issue of six decks' affecting the player's advantage is taken up in a later question.)

Question (F.B.E.): With a running count of +10, are your chances for a win the same with one deck as with four decks? Answer: No. The true count is a more exact measure of your chances of winning. In the beginning of a four-deck shoe, a running count of +10 would equal a true count of 2.5 (running count divided by remaining decks equal true count, e.g., $^{10}/_4 = 2.5$). This same +10 would equate to a true count of +10 early in a one-deck game ($^{10}/_1 = 10$) yielding a much higher player advantage.

Question (G.K.L.): Does a minus count or plus count favor the player? At what point should a player increase his bet? Please clarify examples of running-count bets. Answer: A plus count favors the player. In Atlantic City most of the games are six decks so you shouldn't start increasing your bet significantly until the running count reaches +4. If you are playing with a $500 bankroll, your minimum bet is $2 and your maximum is $10.

Question (E.U.): Your review of eleven popular blackjack books* indicates point-count systems similar to each other which I suspect are all superfluous and unnecessary. Could you not get roughly equivalent results merely by watching the 10s and aces? For example: Simply expect an average of six or seven 10s and one or two aces for each hand. If fewer than six 10s are played, then you obviously have a plus count. A rough approximation can be estimated for the remaining decks as you go along. While this may not be technically or mathematically accurate, it does not matter as each of the eleven books will result in a different point-count anyway. Answer: If you are going to count, you must count correctly and accurately. Otherwise your information is worthless and will not provide you with a winning advantage. There are 10-count systems that you can play and, although not as accurate as point-count systems, will provide you with a winning edge if you play them accurately. You cannot win at blackjack by using "rough approximations."

As far as the point-count systems are concerned, Reader E.U. is correct from the viewpoint of the occasional gambler. There is just not that much difference among the systems described in my review of the eleven popular blackjack books. The occasional gambler should use one that is simple to play—the High-Low System discussed earlier in this chapter.

Question (M.B.): By following the advice in your column in the *Atlantic City Press,* I have been winning modestly at blackjack. I play about once a week. I would like to win a little more money, but I don't know when to

---

*For details on this review, see Chapter 17.

bet heavy and when to bet light. Should I bet heavy when
many face cards have been played? Or wait until the
remaining deck contains most of the face cards? Answer:
You have the advantage when the remaining deck is rich
in 10s, face cards and aces. That's when you should
increase your bet. I recommend that you learn High-Low
as described earlier in this chapter—but if you don't wish
to invest the time, try the following simple Ten-Count
System.:

10s Seen	Remaining Decks	Betting Strategy
9 or fewer	5 or fewer	See below
26 or fewer	4 or fewer	
44 or fewer	3 or fewer	
61 or fewer	2 or fewer	

You play this system by counting 10s and watching the
discard tray. When *five* or fewer decks remain to be played
(one deck has been dealt), you increase your bet if you
have counted five or fewer 10-value cards. When *four* or
fewer decks remain to be played, you increase your bet if
twenty-six or fewer 10-value cards have been counted.
When *three* or fewer decks have been played, bet up if 44
or fewer 10s have been counted. And when *two* or fewer
decks remain to be played, bet up when 61 or fewer 10s
have been counted.

The amount you increase your bet is determined by
your bankroll and the number of 10s counted. The fewer
the 10s for each remaining deck value, the more you want
to bet. Remember, however, never bet more than one-
fiftieth of your bankroll on any given hand.

Caution: This system is not as effective as the High-Low System discussed earlier in this chapter. Your long-run advantage is about 0.5% compared to 1-1.5% for High-Low.

Play the same way for *three* decks remaining and *two* decks remaining.

Question (R.H.): I am looking for a good Advanced Blackjack System to use on a full-time basis. What is your general opinion of advanced point-count systems vs. simple point-count systems, and which advanced system should I use? Answer: You don't need an advanced blackjack system to win at blackjack. True, you may derive a slightly higher *theoretical* advantage by using an advanced system, but this is usually nullified in actual play by higher player-error rates and shorter playing duration because of more intense concentration required. I recommend that you use High-Low. It is the system I use and teach in my BLACKJACK CLINIC. To my knowledge, it is used by more blackjack players than any other system.

Question (G.B.): Is it worth the time and effort to learn an advanced point-count system and play against six decks (the Atlantic City game)? There has been little written on the subject of six-deck blackjack games. I have read Humble's *Blackjack/Gold* and he does not recommend playing against six decks. Can you beat the six-deck game? What preparations are needed? Answer: You can beat the six-deck Atlantic City game. You do not need an advanced point-count system—you can win with High-Low. The disadvantages of a six-deck game are a 0.05% reduction in basic strategy (to 0.2%) and about 25 to 30% fewer high-count betting opportunities. You have to wait longer to get your high-count betting opportunities but you still get enough of them to yield a 1 to 1.5% advantage.

To understand this six-deck phenomenon in simple terms, assume that four 10s and one ace have been seen out of the first deck played. Your winning advantage is dependent upon the remaining 10s and aces to be played compared to the number of remaining decks. Here is the effect of these five high cards (four 10s, one ace dealt) in a two-deck, four-deck and six-deck game.

	Decks Played	Decks Remaining	% of 10s/aces remaining to be played
Two-Deck Game	1	1	67%
Four-Deck Game	1	3	48%
Six-Deck Game	1	5	44%

What this table proves is that five high cards played do not produce a remaining deck worth as much in a six-deck as in a four-deck game or two-deck game. Therefore, you have to wait longer for favorable situations in a six-deck game.

This table also suggests that the percentage of 10s and aces remaining to be played begins to level off as the number of decks increases. This is true. In a hypothetical eight-deck game this percentage is 43. In a hypothetical 25-deck game, the percentage is 40.

Chapter 6
Key to Success: Money Management

Card-counting techniques have been generally known for about the past twenty years—ever since the publication of Ed Thorp's *Beat the Dealer*.

There are more than fifty point-count systems available—some so complicated that they are usable only by experts; others so simple that they are usable by almost anyone. If most gamblers know that it is possible to achieve an advantage over the casino, why then are casino blackjack profits increasing faster than the number of players?

The major reason is money management. Many blackjack players are excellent card counters but they lose because they overbet in proportion to their bankroll. It never ceases to amaze me that a counter will spend hours developing his or her skills and then walk into a casino with a $500 bankroll and make $25 bets.

If you play High-Low as described in the last chapter, your overall advantage is around 1%. This isn't much and you may have many losing sessions before your 1% advantage prevails. Your objective is to bet the correct proportion of your bankroll to minimize your chances of going broke. You want to "grind out" the casino like they grind out all the losing gamblers.

HANDLING YOUR EMOTIONS AND DEVELOPING WINNING ATTITUDES

Even the serious blackjack player sometimes has problems keeping his emotions in check when playing blackjack.

I will use a recent experience of my own to make this point. I was playing in the Resorts Casino in Atlantic City, betting $25 to $500 and playing about even after a couple of hours of play. All of a sudden the running count reached +20. With a little over two decks remaining, this is an extremely favorable situation—I had about a 5% advantage. This means that on the average I will win about 52.5 times out of 100 for these types of hands.

Since I was getting very little heat, I decided to play two hands of $500 each. The first hand, I was dealt a pair of 6s; the second a 10. The dealer showed a 3. I split the 6s and pulled an ace to the first split hand—a soft 17 vs. a

3—clearly a double-down situation. I doubled and pulled a 6 for a total of 13. I pulled a 10 to the second 6. I now had a total of $1500 riding on this hand.

On the second hand, I doubled the 10 and pulled a 5— not a very good total, but with the dealer showing a 3, I wasn't too worried. I now had a total of $2500 riding on the two hands!

The dealer turned over a 2 for a total of 5 and hit her hand with a 10 for a 15. I'm beginning to feel comfortable with the impending break when the next card she turns over is a 2—a lowly 17 wipes out my $2500. A $5000 swing! Instead of picking up $5000 (a $2500 bet plus a $2500 win), I watched her quickly scoop up my $2500 bet. I played a few more hands but I had lost my edge. I still was thinking back to that hand. Shaken by the experience, I quit for the day and went home.

There is an obvious lesson in this story. DO NOT PLAY BLACKJACK WHEN YOU BECOME EMOTIONALLY INVOLVED OR EMOTIONALLY UPSET.

If

- You think the dealer is hot,

- You think the table is cold,

- You are tempted to overbet,

- You lose some hands you "should have won,"

- Other players are making decisions that are upsetting you,

• You are losing the count or think you are losing the count,

• You have lost your session bankroll,

STOP PLAYING!

If you live close to the casino, go home. You can always return another day.

If you have traveled a distance for a weekend or vacation, take a long break—at least two hours and preferably three or four. Do something to get your mind off blackjack like eating, sleeping, being entertained or visiting a place of interest.

Review the characteristics of a successful blackjack player listed below. Form a picture of yourself in your mind with these characteristics. Visualize yourself as a winner. See yourself accumulating chips and playing with a calm and cool attitude. If you feel like a winner, you will play with more confidence and will keep a more accurate running count.

Never, never go to the casino with the idea that you have so much money that you can "afford to lose." Always go with the full confidence that you will win. Put these attitudes in your mind and make your winning postulates on the way to the casino. If you start losing them while playing, take a break as described above.

CHARACTERISTICS of A SuCCESSful BlackjACk PlAYER Vs. A GAMblER

Successful Blackjack Player	Gambler Who Plays Blackjack
Has the confidence and attitude that he can win	
Never overbets	Overbets in relation to his bankroll
Raises his bet only when the count is right	
Never deviates from the basic strategy (with the exception of planned variations with the true count)	If he loses, makes a series of large bets in an attempt to recoup
	Makes hunch plays even though he knows the basic strategy
Plays calm, cool and detached; if he gets emotionally involved, quits for a break or for the day	Gets highly excited (perhaps with sweaty palms) when he anticipates his next trip to the casino
Never gambles with money he can't afford to lose; keeps a separate gambling bankroll	Gambles with money he can't afford to lose; keeps no separate gambling bankroll

| Plans his trips to the casino for enjoyment and relaxation; never to get even | Schedules an early return trip to win back his money from the casino |

PLAYER POLICIES FOR MONEY MANAGEMENT

• Set aside your casino bankroll as a separate "kitty" or fund. Keep it in a separate checking account or safe deposit box.

• Divide your casino bankroll by 50. This is the size of your maximum bet. For example, if your casino bankroll is $500, your maximum bet size is $10. This may sound like a small amount but by following this axiom, you will virtually never go broke. If $10 is your maximum bet, your bet variations will range from $2 to $10 at a $2 table.

• Don't drink anything containing alcohol while you play. If at all possible, you should not drink any alcohol for twenty-hours before playing because it takes this long for the effects to totally wear off. In other words, for best results and to play at your full mental capacity, you should not drink at all while playing blackjack.

• Keep a detailed record of your winnings and losses. Record your emotional frame of mind and how well you were counting. If you make any mistakes, make a mental note of them and record them in your records.

- You should vary your maximum bet as your casino bankroll varies, e.g.:

Casino bankroll	Max. bet
$1000	$20
900	18
800	16
500	10
1500	30
2000	40
2500	50

FACTORS THAT AFFECT YOUR WINNINGS

Your long-run advantage varies between 1 and 1.5% depending on the following factors:

- Rules of play (e.g., favorable rules such as doubling down after split, and surrender, increase your advantage);

- Betting spread, e.g., varying from $2 to $15 on plus counts is better than varying between $5 to $15;

- Number of players at table—the fewer the better. When the deck is rich in 10s and aces, you are dealt more favorable hands if there are fewer players;

- Number of hands played per unit time. This is definitely dependent on the previous factor but also depends on the speed of the dealer;

- The shuffle point—the farther down the cards are dealt before the dealer shuffles, the more favorable your odds of winning;

- Number of decks—the fewer decks you play with, the more favorable your odds.

Some of these factors you can influence and others you can't. Your objective is to find and play in an optimum environment where you can optimize the above factors, or to set limits on the factors to conform to the environment you're playing in.

COMMENTS ON THE BETTING SPREAD

The betting spread (the ratio between your maximum and minimum bet) that you use is a function of your casino environment and their attitude toward card counters. In Atlantic City, the conditions are very favorable toward nonprofessional card counters (currently professional blackjack players can be barred). I use a 12 to 1 ratio and am not bothered at all. In most casinos in the Caribbean, you can get away with a spread of 10 to 1 or higher.

The Nevada casinos, however, are a horse of a different color. Most players do not use a spread of greater than 4 to 1 unless they play two hands—then they get an effective 8 to 1 spread, e.g., betting $5 units they bet $20 on each of two hands in favorable situations. The 4 to 1 spread is not really 4 to 1 because to avoid the characteristics of a card counter, you progress to 4 to 1 by first betting two units and then four if the deck is still favorable.

BETTING AND BANKROLL STRATEGIES

In order to win at blackjack, you must bet more when the count is plus. In order not to get wiped out on a bad run of cards, you must never bet more than one-fiftieth of your entire bankroll.

Here are some examples of how to bet for various-sized bankrolls. In my BLACKJACK CLINIC I start students on a unique but simple betting system, then assist them to progress to a money management strategy that fits their bankroll, temperament and degree of risk they wish to take.

1. Progessive Betting with the Running Count (Casino bankroll = $500)

	Bet Size	Running Count
	$ 2 or $3	Minus to +4
$2 or $3 Table	5	+4 or +8
	10	+8 or greater

2. Progessive Betting with the Running Count (Casino bankroll = $1000)

	Bet Size	Running Count
$2 or $3 Table	$ 2 or $3	Minus to +4
	5	+5 to +7
	10	+8 to +10
	20	+11 or higher
$5 Table	$ 5	Minus to +4
	10	+4 to +8
	20	+9 or higher

3. Progressive Betting with the Running Count (Casino bankroll = $2500)

	Bet Size	Running Count
$5 table	$ 5	Minus to +4
	10	+5
	15	+6
	20	+7
	25	+8
	30	+9
	35	+10
	40	+11
	45	+12
	50	+13 or higher

For the above progressive strategies, you should choose one that fits your bankroll, the casino playing conditions and your temperament. If you are a conservative bettor, progress as slowly as $2, 5, 10, 20; if you are aggressive and can get away with it, progress from $2 to 20 as long as the running count is +4 or higher.

Money Management Axioms

1. You can win at blackjack only if you learn how to avoid going broke. Short-run losses can kill the best card-counter in the world unless he knows how to bet in proportion to his bankroll. A proper betting method is the only way to achieve the long-run advantage of 1 to 1.5% of your total action.

2. Bet Variation with the point count yields 85% of your advantage. Basic strategy variations provide the other 15% but are usually too complicated for the beginning to intermediate blackjack player to attempt. Therefore, maximize your betting spread when conditions permit. You increase your advantage by betting from $2 to $20 (10 to 1 spread) instead of $5 to $20 (4 to 1 spread) if you are playing with a $1000 bankroll.

Many people who write to me in care of my weekly casino gaming column do not count cards and use a progressive betting strategy. Although I attempt to convince these readers that card counting is the only way to win at blackjack in the long run, I do give advice on progressive betting systems to those readers who decide not to learn card counting. The questions and answers below deal with progressive betting systems.

QUESTIONS AND ANSWERS

Question (G.L.): Does a betting strategy of doubling your bet after each loss until you get a win and then returning to your original bet work? If I never hit a breaking hand, then eventually the dealer will break and my last bet will recoup all of my prior losses and give me a profit equal to my original bet. I start out betting $10 and raise my next bet to $20, $40, $80, etc., until I reach the maximum bet for that particular table and hoping I have drawn a good hand or the dealer has gone over 21. Answer: This betting strategy is a very dangerous way to play blackjack. I have seen periods of play where the dealer would go many hands in succession without breaking. I once played at a table where the dealer went through 2 four-deck shoes without breaking—approximately sixteen straight hands. I lost every one of these hands except one. I once played at a table in Las Vegas where I lost twenty-two consecutive hands. Now it is possible that Reader G.L. could use this strategy for two or three sessions, or even five or six times or more without losing. But there will come a point where he will either reach the table maximum bet or lose his entire bankroll. For example, with a $500 bankroll and starting with a $10 bet, it would take only five straight losses to lose $310 ($10 + 20 + 40 + 80 + 160 = 310). The next bet should be $620, but he wouldn't have the bankroll to cover it.

Question (P.H.): When is the best time to increase your bet—when you are winning or losing? (B.A.) Should you set a goal as to what your winnings will be or quit when you feel the cards are no longer running your way? Answer: The answer to the first question is to increase your bet when you are winning (assuming you are not counting cards). This will be further discussed below.

The answer to the second question is to set a goal for your winnings and quit when you achieve this goal. Or you could set a stop loss of, say, 20% of your winnings and quit if and when you reach the stop loss. If you feel the cards are not running with you, you should quit and not chase your money. You should have a loss limit and quit when you reach this limit.

Question (J.K.): Would you evaluate the following progressive betting system for blackjack?

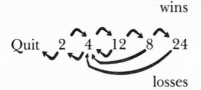

wins

Quit   2   4   12   8   24

losses

Starting with four units, the arrows on top tell which way to go on a win. The arrows on bottom tell where to go on a loss.

Question (J.B.): I play $5 blackjack and progress, when winning, as follows: $5, $10, $15, $25, $35, $50, $75, $100, $150, $200, $300 and $350 to infinity. While I realize that this progression will always result in my losing my largest bet, when I lose that bet I will have in front of me a profit of *more than that bet* on that particular series. This is not true early in the progression, but it is true after seven or eight wins, and it's these longer streaks that one is seeking . . . I only wish to ask what you think of my betting progression, and if not in total agreement with it, I would appreciate your thoughts on how to improve it.

Question (W.G.J., III): Playing basic strategy, we have found we can play the house about even. It seems to us that in order to be a winner at blackjack, some kind of betting system must be used. We have tried many systems: win progression, loss progression, doubling the bet on wins and losses and many others. Do you know of a betting system that is as good as the basic strategy?

Answers to the above three questions: Gamblers have been developing betting systems to try to overcome the casino advantage for hundreds of years. For example, the Martingale System (doubling up after each successive loss until a win is achieved) was devised in the late 1700s.

It can be proven mathematically that no betting system can be formulated that will overcome the house advantage. In the case of blackjack there is no progressive betting system that will improve the basic-strategy player's advantage of 0.2%. When I first started to gamble I didn't believe the mathematicians and played over two million hands on the computer to test the effect of various betting systems on the casino advantage. The results proved that betting systems have no effect on the casino advantage, so I believed the mathematicians and learned how to count cards.

The optimum method for varying your bet in the game of blackjack is to count cards. When the odds favor the house, you make a minimum bet. When the odds favor you, you make a large bet.

My caveats presented above notwithstanding, progressive betting systems will work—when you are lucky. They do not work when you are unlucky. Therefore, if you do not wish to learn how to count cards, I recommend using a progressive system based on a series of wins in succession—not a series of losses in succession.

There is a multitude of these systems around. You have to pick one or develop one that fits your style of betting. If you are feeling lucky and decide to bet fairly aggressively, you could use a system similar to Reader J.K.'s. He increases his bet rapidly but plays for only four wins in succession. If you wish to bet more conservatively, you could use the following progression:

After first win—bet 2 units; second win—bet 4; third, 5; fourth, 5; fifth, 5; sixth, 5; seventh, 10; eighth, 15; ninth, 20; tenth, 25; next, 30. A unit is your basic bet size; e.g., $2 equals one unit.

This progression is aggressive for the first two winning hands as the bet is doubled each time. Then it becomes conservative as profits are built up to finance a potential doubling-down or pair-splitting situation. Ten wins in succession with this progression would yield a profit of 67 units (assuming no bets doubled or no blackjacks) in

addition to a 30-unit bet for the next hand. Remember to
return to a one-unit bet when the series is interrupted by
a loss.

A streak of 10 wins in succession will occur about once
in each 4000 hands played. If you don't want to wait that
long, play a simple and very conservative progression like
this, 1, 2, 3, 1, 2, 3, etc. Each three hands won in
succession will generate a profit of six units.

Better yet, develop a progressive betting system to suit
your own style of play. To do this, make three columns on
a piece of paper with the following headings: Hand
Number; Units Bet; Cumulative Profit (after winning
hand and placing next bet).

For each winning hand in succession decide on the units
you will bet. That is your progression. Use simple arith-
metic or poker chips to figure out the cumulative profit
for each step in the series. If your units increase rapidly,
you are betting aggressively and going for the big kill. The
disadvantage of an aggressive progression is that too
much of the profits are lost if the series is interrupted by
an early loss. A conservative progression, with the units
bet increasing less rapidly, would prevent this from
happening. You do, however, win less money on the
longer winning streaks.

To minimize your chances of going broke, be sure to
take along sufficient capital. I recommend at least 200
units for a conservative progression and 400 to 500 for an
aggressive progression.

CHAPTER 7
CASINO COMPORTMENT

When you start blackjack as a counter, you will draw a lot more attention from the pit bosses and floor personnel who monitor the play at several blackjack tables enclosing a pit. They do not like card counters because they believe that all card counters win money from casinos. If they spot you as a counter, their tactics to keep you from winning money include everything from showing you a lot of attention (heat) to barring you from play.

Here are some tips to keep from being recognized as a card counter.

1. Watch your betting spread (the ratio between your maximum bet and minimum bet). If you jump right from a $5 bet to a $50 bet, the pit boss will know right away that you are a counter. Progress with the count and hold your bet increases to 2 or 3 to 1 over the prior hand.

2. Try to limit yourself to one hour's play per pit and no more than two hours per casino. If you think the pit boss has spotted you as a counter, get up and walk away without looking back.

3. Be aware of *when* to place your bet. If you wait too long, it will appear that you are waiting to get the count before putting out your money. Put your bet out as quickly as possible after getting the count.

4. Be aware of when the dealer is going to shuffle the deck, so you will not have a big bet out and then see your favorable situation get shuffled away. Don't push your big bet out if the cut card is the next card to be dealt from the shoe. You could always take it back, but this is very noticeable. I would advise getting up and walking away the second time if you get caught with a big bet out when the dealer shuffles.

5. Don't change your bet after a push if the count drops.

6. Vary your bet at the top of the shoe.

7. Try not to be the biggest bettor at your table.

8. If you are winning, move some of your winning chips into your coat pocket. Do this when no casino personnel are looking.

9. Don't change your small denomination chips for larger denomination chips ("changing color") at the table at the end of your session. If you do this, the pit boss will know how much you have won.

10. Don't turn your head side to side when counting.

11. Don't move your lips.

12. Don't strain to see the cards at opposite ends of the table. Don't strain to see the cut card or bottom card.

13. Act natural. Smile and be friendly. Talk to the other players. Compliment the third-base player when he

makes the "right" decision and the dealer breaks. Frown when someone splits a pair of tens (many players regard this as bad luck). Say "nice hit" when a player draws to a stiff and makes 20 or 21.

14. Talk to the dealer. Ask if she's been hot when you sit down. Make a small bet for her early in your session ($1-2) if you are playing $5 or less as your minimum bet.

15. Don't be afraid of floorpersons or pit bosses. If one wanders by your table or stops and watches, don't assume he's spotted you for a counter. Continue to play your game and make your bets. If he stops longer than usual start making flat bets or get up at an appropriate time and leave the table.

16. When you leave the casino, don't stop at the cashier's cage on the way out. Try to cash your chips in at different hours than when you're playing. This rule can be flexible if you're only playing occasionally.

Casino Comportment Axioms

Play like a loser and look like a loser. Don't get too greedy at any one casino—spread your play around. Never offer advice at the table. Accept all advice offered in a friendly manner but use none of it. Go along with all the blackjack myths. Act natural, not nervous or intense. Get as much of your attention off the cards as possible.

SECTION III

Atlantic City Blackjack Rules— Casinos and Counters Wage an Ongoing War

Section Overview

In Chapter 8, the interested reader will find a short history of the Atlantic City blackjack rules and how the rules were changed to allow the casinos to bar professional card counters. Chapter 9 relates the story of the New Jersey Casino Control Commission's thirteen-day experiment in December of 1979 to allow professional card counters to return to play. In Chapter 10 the complex issue of whether or not card counters should be barred is discussed. Chapter 11 examines the present status and answers the question: Can the Atlantic City blackjack game still be beaten by a skilled card counter?

CHAPTER 8

A Short History of the Atlantic City Blackjack Rules and the Barring Incident in January 1979

Barred. The dreaded word was uttered to twenty-two blackjack card counters on Tuesday and Wednesday, January 30 and 31. The Resorts Casino crumbled under the pressure of a number of professional blackjack players' heavy winnings and, with a loophole in the State Casino Gaming regulations found by Commissioner Lordi, told the counters that their presence at the blackjack tables would no longer be tolerated.

Stories about the barring incident were carried in

several area newspapers and generated a tremendous amount of interest in blackjack—the only game where the gambler can actually gain an advantage against the casino.

The occasional gambler is asking some fundamental questions about the incident that need to be answered: What does card counting mean and how difficult is it to master? Why were the counters barred? If I learn how to count cards and start winning at blackjack, could I be barred?

In order to answer these questions it is necessary to understand the issues surrounding the barring incident and briefly review the short history of blackjack in Atlantic City.

Due largely to the efforts of Commissioner Albert Merck, the Resorts Casino opened on May 26, 1978, with some of the most favorable blackjack rules of any casino in the world. A player is allowed to double his bet on any two cards which he is dealt. Many casinos restrict a player's doubling decision to hands totaling 10 or 11 only. The player is also allowed to double his bet after splitting any pair of like cards. For example, if a player is dealt a pair of 8s, splits them and draws a 3 to the first 8, he may double his bet in return for taking only one more card.

The Atlantic City rule that really caught the attention of serious blackjack players is called Early Surrender. If the player is dealt two cards he doesn't like, he is allowed to surrender his hand in return for giving up half his bet. But, unlike Las Vegas, since the dealer doesn't check his hole-card until after all the players' hands have been played, the astute player can surrender, especially when the dealer shows an ace or a 10, before the dealer ascertains that he has a blackjack (a blackjack is any 10-value card and ace and is an automatic winner).

Knowing when to surrender plus the other favorable rules give the basic strategy player a small advantage (about 0.2%) over the casino even without counting cards.

The attention of the blackjack world also focused on Atlantic City because, in the beginning, the State regulations were interpreted to protect the counters and disallow the casino from barring them. The casino was allowed to move the cut card (the card placed in the shoe to determine when the four or six decks will be reshuffled) toward the front of the shoe and thus give the counters fewer chances for a favorable deck (a favorable deck is a deck rich in 10s and aces and with the odds of winning favoring the counter). Any time the casino suspected a player of counting, they would move the cut card to the halfway point or even to within one deck of the front of the shoe.

Against known professionals, the casino also could shuffle or threaten to shuffle after every hand to eliminate the counter's advantage. The casino was allowed to shuffle the shoe when they changed dealers, so the dealer was changed before the play of each hand.

All this changed on January 4 when, due again to the efforts of Commissioner Merck, the State Casino Control Commission prohibited the casinos from placing the cut card more than one-third the distance from the back of the shoe and from arbitrarily shuffling the shoe by changing dealers more than once an hour.

The Resorts Casino reacted immediately to the rule change. They eliminated the $100 minimum bet tables and reduced the $25 to $1000 tables to $5 to $300 if they suspected a counter at work. Additional countermeasures such as not allowing a player to play two hands and requiring a player to play every hand (some counters would sit out a hand or two if the odds were not in their favor) were also put into effect.

Casino management also instituted surveillance procedures for suspected card counters. Security guards began keeping an eye on Ken Uston, for example, the moment he walked into the casino. (An amusing incident that Uston related to me was a game of "hide and seek" he played with the security guards. Knowing they were watching him, he ducked upstairs and hid among the nickel slot machines. Then, surreptitiously, he leaned over the railing and watched the security men scurry around the casino, checking with each other on their walkie-talkies—looking all over for him.)

The casino management also began filming card counters in action. These films and other evidence were taken to the Casino Control Commission after the professional blackjack teams arrived and began winning large sums of money.

The salient parts of Commissioner Lordi's letter interpreting the State regulations to allow Resorts to bar the counters are as follows:

"There is nothing in the act or the Commission regulations that would prohibit a casino from excluding professional card counters from its casino . . . the Commission, however, would not sanction the exclusion of players who are simply skilled or lucky under the guise of excluding them as professional card counters . . ."

The occasional gambler, then, does not have to worry about being barred from play at the Resorts or other Atlantic City casinos.

The issue is whether or not you are a professional—actually make your living playing the game. The issue is also whether or not a professional has the right to play. The professionals assert that their civil liberties are being infringed upon and that they are barred simply because they are winning. The casinos, on the other hand, are in business to make a profit and look with a jaundiced eye upon anything which threatens to reduce those profits.

This issue is still unresolved in the Nevada casinos. Ken Uston, for example, has lawsuits pending against at least eight Nevada casinos.

After the January 31 barring incident Ken initiated legal action against the Resorts Casino and against the New Jersey Casino Control Commission for preventing him from playing and earning a livelihood.

Ken's legal actions were mainly responsible for a thirteen-day experiment conducted in December 1979 to allow the professional card counters to return to play. I documented the history of this thirteen-day experiment in an article written for *Sports Form* and published on January 5, 1980. This article is included as Chapter 9.

Chapter 9

Card Counters KO Casinos in Thirteen-Day Blackjack Test*

Professional card counters beat the new blackjack rules put into effect as an experiment in Atlantic City casinos in December 1979.

According to figures gathered by the New Jersey Casino Control Commission, the counters cost Atlantic City's two open casinos about $1.4 million dollars during the thirteen days the new rules were in effect.

Michael A. Santeniello, the commission's assistant director for licensing, said the State's attempt to allow professional card counters to play blackjack cost the casinos approximately $110,000 a day. The impact of the coun-

*Reprinted with permission of *Sports Form,* PO Box 15205, Las Vegas, NV 89114

ters was so great that both casinos reported a net loss at the blackjack tables for one day during the experiment, he said.

The professional counters were again barred from play on December 13—thirteen days after the Great Experiment began.

Ken Uston, a professional counter whose legal actions against the Atlantic City casinos were mainly responsible for the thirteen-day experiment allowing the counters to return to play, said the estimates of how much the casinos lost was "pure hogwash."

"I think the figures are overstated. I don't know exactly why," Uston said. "In some instances I think the Casino Commission was not given accurate figures (by the casinos)."

The Casino Control Commission spent about six months in designing the experimental blackjack rules. They felt that the new rules would equalize the game and make it possible for all players to play—card counters and occasional gamblers—without deleteriously affecting the casinos' win rates. The rules put into effect were as follows:

1. A dealer may shuffle up if one of the following conditions occurs:
   a. At a $2, $5 or $10 minimum bet table, if a player raises his bet by 5 to 1 over the immediately preceding bet (e.g., from $5 to $25).
   b. At a $2, $5 or $10 table if a new player enters in the middle of a shoe and bets $100 or more.
   c. At a $25 or $100 minimum table if a player raises his bet by 3 to 1 over the immediately preceding bet (e.g., from $100 to $300).

    d. At a $25 or $100 minimum table if a player enters the game in the middle of a shoe and bets $200 or more.

In actual operation the dealer did not make a shuffle-up decision. A floorperson monitored the bets and called over a pit boss, who made the decision.

2. The casinos were given the right to place the cut card marking the shuffle point in the middle of the stack. A prior rule required them to deal two-thirds of the shoe. In the six-deck shoe used in the Atlantic City casinos, this rule allowed dealing only three decks to the player instead of the former four.

The impact of this rule was many lost betting opportunities when the count was high and then the shoe was broken and the cards were reshuffled at the halfway point. The professional card counters overcame this disadvantage by betting large sums of money sooner. Large bankrolls make this possible with little risk of their going broke.

More than 100 card counters previously barred from play in January of 1979 descended upon the Resorts International and Boardwalk Regency casinos when the above rules were implemented.

On Saturday, December 8, the rules were further tightened because of reported heavy counter winnings. Players were limited to 2 to 1 increase in their bet size on successive hands at $25-and-up tables and a 3 to 1 increase at the lower minimum-bet tables. If these limits were violated, the casino had the right to reshuffle. This change was put into effect mainly to stymie the professionals from increasing their bets too rapidly on favorable counts. This change had little effect on amateur counters, who seldom raised their bets by this amount anyway—even if they did the casino pit bosses were not overly concerned and did not order the shoe to be shuffled. This was because their bets were very small relative to the bet sizes the professionals were putting into play.

The third change approved by the Casino Control Commission before the rules were scrapped on December 13 stopped the professionals from "back counting." Back counting is standing behind the table, counting, and then jumping into play when the count is favorable. The counter leaves the table when the count returns to a minus condition and the odds favor the casino. This rule, too, was put into effect to stymie the professionals. I heard no reports from amateur counters or occasional players who were stopped from playing until the shuffle point was reached.

The thirteen-day experiment produced some interesting scenes in the Atlantic City casinos.

Young, modish-looking guys dressed in jeans and sneakers sitting at the $100 tables with stacks of $100 and $500 chips in front of them; leaving the tables with five or six racks of chips when the count goes negative; team meetings and animated conversations in the aisles as counters decide to increase or decrease their maximum bets depending on how much they've won or lost.

Many of the professionals back-counted the $25 tables waiting for favorable counts before they would sit down to play. Three or four counters would gather at one table, sit down together, play a few hands and then all leave simultaneously when the count went negative.

Of course, Uston, the guy who was mainly responsible for the experiment, was there and in style. Uston always drew a crowd when he played. Huge amounts of black and purple ($500) chips were piled carelessly in front of him. There was usually a stack of $100 bills nestled among the chips. A Krugerrand laid carelessly on top of an unneeded pile of green chips.

When the experiment ended on December 13, the pre-December 1 rules were reinstituted: the casinos must deal two-thirds of a shoe, players may bet whatever they wish (up to the maximum) and only professional card counters are barred from play.

What constitutes a professional? This is the next policy issue that the New Jersey Control Commission must grapple with in the never-ending battle between the counters and the casinos.

CHAPTER 10
SHOULD CARD COUNTERS BE BARRED FROM PLAY?

Why is blackjack the most popular casino table game? Why did Nevada casino blackjack revenues increase from $59 million to $395 million during the years 1967-77? Why are casino blackjack profits increasing faster than the number of blackjack players and 50% faster than profits from the other casino games?

The answers to these questions are obvious. Because blackjack is a game of skill, not a game of chance. Even without card counting there is skill involved in deciding whether to hit, stand, surrender, double-down or split pairs. Players enjoy the skill involved even if they make their decisions by hunch instead of by mathematical and computer derived rules.

The second answer is that most players know that blackjack is the only game where they can actually gain an advantage over the casino. They have heard about the professional card counters who have won millions of dollars and who beat the casinos consistently. They want to take a shot and get in on the action. They've read a book or two and don't realize that a high degree of skill is required which involves discipline, patience and practice. Even though they know the game can be beaten, most players just do not make the commitment to develop the requisite skills and play against a casino advantage of about 6%. Or they take a shot with a limited bankroll and get wiped out.

If there were no card counting and card counters, if the rules were changed so blackjack were a game of chance like craps, roulette and baccarat and not a game of skill, then the popularity of the game would fall off and none of the presently opened casinos would continue to expand their blackjack tables with the expectation of reaping larger profits.

If card counters are indirectly contributing to casino profits, why, then, are some of them barred from play? Whether or not professional card counters have the right to play is an issue that has perplexed casino management and the New Jersey Casino Control Commission, not to mention the professional blackjack players themselves, since the casinos opened.

The most recent major barring incidents occurred at the termination of the thirteen-day experiment in December 1979 in which the commission tried to tighten up the rules of play and make it tougher for the professionals to win. The reported casino win reduction during the thir-teen days approached $1.4 million, so the experiment was dropped and the counters were once again barred.

Let's get back to our original question and the crux of this chapter. Why are professional card counters barred from play? There is also the corollary question: Should nonprofessional or amateur card counters be barred from play? One casino manager told me that the situation is similar to the proprietor of a grocery store. Some custom-ers come in and pay 65¢ for a loaf of bread. Others come in and get the same loaf free or are paid to take the loaf home with them. Casino management's viewpoint is that they simply cannot afford to offer a game to anyone who beats them consistently. The players retort that with all their millions of profit, why can't they afford it? The casinos reply that they have a business, stockholders and a bottom line to manage.

What is the solution, if any? The first thing that should be done is to define exactly what constitutes a professional card counter. At the present time, the casinos are not supposed to bar anyone who is *not* a professional card counter. However, because of the lack of a standard in this area, casino management has taken some liberty with this regulation and barred many players who under no circumstances could be considered professionals.

An interesting example, which made the front page of the *Atlantic City Press* on Wednesday, January 30, 1980, was the barring of the Diamond brothers by the Board-walk Regency. One brother, a staff reporter for the *Press,* is a $5 player and was ahead $42 when the barring occurred. The other brother is not a card counter, was betting with his hunches and was enjoying a lucky streak when the barring incident took place. There is no way that either of these two gentlemen could be considered professional card counters, but the Regency got away with the barring because of the lack of a standard.

Here are three criteria which could be used to define a professional card counter: (1) one who makes his living from the game and has no other visible means of support; (2) one who has reported blackjack winnings on his federal income tax for any of the past three years; (3) one who is a self-proclaimed expert through playing, writing and instructing.

If the casinos are given the right to bar professionals, they could not bar the counter for more than thirty days without giving the counter, through the commission, a chance to disprove the allegation. The counter could produce evidence of a full-time job (one that he was working at prior to getting barred) and evidence of no reported blackjack winnings on his federal income tax returns. If this evidence is acceptable, the counter can return to play.

As an alternative to barring, the commission could use a computer study to define a set of rules that would apply only to professionals. Special tables for the professionals could be set up where these rules would be in effect. This is, in effect, what was happening during the recent thirteen-day experiment. The 2 to 1 parlay bet limitation and the prevention of a "back counter" from sitting down to play until the shuffle point were used by the casino pit bosses against known professionals only.

I don't agree with barring professionals, but this action

has been a fact of life for the past fifteen years. I know many professionals who have never been barred. Many play at Atlantic City and get little or no heat. The casinos don't even know of their existence and many never suspect them of being card counters. On the other hand, some casino managers have developed a highly trained eye for spotting counters but allow some suspected professionals to play as long as they don't play too long or win too much. What is the difference between these professionals and those that have been barred in Atlantic City? Bankroll size, amount of money won and the counter's casino comportment. Many professionals are content to make a reasonable living from the game. They spread their play around—from casino to casino and from area to area. They may play in Nevada one month, Atlantic City the next, and Europe the one after that.

Many of the professionals barred in Atlantic City just did not follow the accepted rules of casino comportment. Playing with large bankrolls, they flaunted their card-counting abilities with no regard to being recognized as a counter or not. Most professionals play in such a way that it is very difficult to recognize them as card counters.

Chapter 11

The Present Status: Can the Atlantic City Game Still Be Beaten by a Skilled Card Counter?

Kenny Uston sued Resorts International for refusing to let him play blackjack and won the case. Resorts appealed to the State Supreme Court and received a stay pending the outcome of the court's decision. If the Supreme Court upholds the appellate decision, all barred card counters will be allowed to play and the casinos will no longer have the right to bar any card counter from playing blackjack.

If this happens, the casinos will petition to the Casino Control Commission to make the game much more difficult to beat and not worth the while for a professional card counter to play. The casinos have already been successful in convincing the commission to eliminate the early surrender decision, and, with the consent of the commission, are presently testing an eight-deck game with a 50% cut card. If the casinos are no longer allowed to bar card counters, this eight-deck game may become standard in Atlantic City.

The commission is also considering another proposal from the casinos—the use of a double shoe to make it more difficult for the counter to know exactly when to raise his bet on the advantageous hands. One of the double shoes would contain six red-backed decks and the other would contain six black-backed decks. The counter would not know which of the two shoes would be used to deal the next hand until after he or she placed the next bet. This would be decided by the dealer, after all the bets had been placed, by pulling a card from the shoe from which the last hand was dealt. This card would be turned over and if it were a red card, e.g., a diamond or a heart, the hand would be dealt from the "red" shoe; if the card were a club or a spade, the hand would be dealt from the "black" shoe. The counters' dilemma would be how much to bet if one shoe were plus and one shoe were minus.

Can either of these two games be beaten by a skilled card counter? The answer is an overwhelming yes. There are four factors involved.

The first factor is competition. Some of the most favorable games in the world are found in the Las Vegas casinos. The reason? Competition. Casino management is vying for the blackjack player's dollar. The same competitive forces will work in the Atlantic City casinos. Those casinos who want to attract the blackjack players, both card counters and non–card counters, will not offer an eight-deck game. They will continue to offer a six-deck game and therefore do a much higher volume of business than those offering the eight-deck game. Given a choice, any blackjack player would choose a six-deck game over an eight-deck game. The same competitive forces will stifle the introduction of the double shoe. Those casinos instituting such a game will lose their players to other casinos that maintain the standard six-deck shoe game.

The other three factors are strategies that the card counter can employ to beat either of these two games. One factor is traditional card-counting techniques. Bet low or don't bet at all when the count is negative or when the count is not high enough to yield a positive player advantage. Bet progressively higher when the count increases and the player's advantage increases commensurately. True, there will not be as many positive player advantages. But the skilled card counter can refine his money management and betting strategy to take advantage of those high counts when they do occur.

Another factor is team play. Many counters work together and call each other in when the count is high. In this way they optimize their playing time by sharing the count and play many, many more hands when they actually have the advantage over the casino. There is no way a casino can foil a well-drilled blackjack team. We teach team play techniques (called Cooperative Card Counting) in my BLACKJACK CLINIC and have had very few problems with our team players' being barred from play.

Either traditional techniques or team play techniques

can be used to beat the proposed double shoe game. A skilled card counter can keep two counts, one for each shoe, as easily as he can keep one. A single counter or a team will watch for those situations where both shoes are positive. There may be fewer hands to play, but on the other hand the positive counts will last longer.

Team play techniques can also be used to keep track of the red and the black cards remaining in each of the two shoes. If one shoe is highly plus and the other is neutral to negative, the counter still may make a higher bet if the count of red or black cards gives him a greater percentage that the plus shoe will be the one the next hand will be dealt from.

The fourth factor in beating either of these two games is a very powerful technique that can be used to beat any blackjack game in the world. It is elegant in its simplicity but it does take quite a bit of practice to employ. I am not willing to disclose it in this book for fear that the casinos may find a way to counteract this strategy. I disclose it only to those trusted BLACKJACK CLINIC graduates who have consented to take a polygraph test.

One day soon the Atlantic City casino managers will realize that they need have no fear of card counters. They should welcome them with open arms, because it is the card counters who have given the game the popularity which it enjoys today. There are few card counters who actually win, and these players will have very little impact on the casinos' bottom line. Most card counters lose because they don't understand the principles of money management; most are gamblers because they bet beyond the limits of their bankroll. They bet too high on the positive counts and wonder what happens to their bank-roll when they hit a losing streak.

Las Vegas casino managers have understood this fact for years and have very few problems with card counters. They are just not as paranoid about this phantom threat as are their Atlantic City counterparts.

If the Atlantic City casino managers would spend as much time on developing and broadening their market base to entice new players to their blackjack tables, their profits would increase much faster than under the present circumstances, in which most of the managers spend most of their time worrying about how to thwart those card counters who are going to lose—in the long run—anyway.

I would love to open a casino and deal a blackjack game to all of the card counters who have been barred from Atlantic City casinos. I would venture a guess that my profit margin would be just as high as any casino open in that city today.

SECTION IV

Blackjack in Nevada

Section Overview

Even though casino gambling has expanded to Atlantic City, Las Vegas is still the gambling capital of the world. One of the most enjoyable parts of a visit to Las Vegas is the opportunity to play single-deck blackjack. Chapter 12 describes the Nevada Single-Deck game and informs you where to find the best games. Chapter 13 instructs you how to count in a single-deck game. Chapter 14 comments on the Nevada Shoe Game and includes a basic strategy matrix which can be tailored to any set of blackjack rules. Chapter 15 describes many practical tips for maximizing your profits in the Las Vegas casinos. Chapter 16 describes my adventures in the Reno/Tahoe casinos.

CHAPTER 12
THE NEVADA SINGLE-DECK GAME

SINGLE-DECK BLACKJACK
IN LAS VEGAS

Most blackjack players know that single-deck blackjack is more favorable to the player than the multideck shoe games used in most Las Vegas casinos. One reason is that the player is dealt more blackjacks in a single-deck game. Another is that more high-count opportunities occur; therefore the counter has the advantage a higher percentage of the time and, theoretically, can earn more money in a single-deck game.

When I first started playing blackjack in the late fifties, all the games were single-deck. Then, there were no card-counting systems and the casinos were not worried about being "taken advantage of."

As card-counting systems increased in number, single-deck games decreased in number.

The number of single-deck games available in Las Vegas casinos was few and far between up until a year or two ago. Then, because of increasing competition, certain managers began getting smart and offering single-deck games. They realized that there are not that many good blackjack players who are capable of taking advantage of single-deck play. These casinos attracted more blackjack players, earned more money and contributed to the expansion of single-deck play.

(It should be noted that the Reno/Tahoe casinos were never that scared of a single-deck game. Although their playing rules are not as liberal, all of the Reno/Tahoe casinos, with one or two exceptions, have maintained their single-deck games over the years).

Here is a partial list of Las Vegas casinos offering single-deck games.

Las Vegas Strip Casinos Offering Single-Deck Blackjack

Circus-Circus, Caesars Palace, Landmark, Sahara, Silver Slipper, Stardust, Castaways.

Las Vegas Downtown Casinos Offering Single-Deck Blackjack

El Cortez, Fremont, Golden Gate, Horseshoe, Nevada.

In order to win at blackjack, you must develop two skills: (1) learn to play the basic strategy perfectly and (2) learn to count cards.

The strategy consists of a series of decisions rules for standing, hitting, doubling down (doubling your bet and taking one more card), splitting pairs (splitting a like pair, e.g., 3-3, playing two hands and doubling your bet), and surrendering (throwing in your hand and giving up half your bet). The strategy is tabulated below.

The basic strategy for Las Vegas single-deck blackjack games was originally derived by Baldwin, Cantey, McDermott and Maisel and published in their book *Playing Blackjack to Win* (W. Barrows, 1957). Thorp, Braun and Wong have refined and improved this strategy over the years and published their versions of it in *Beat the Dealer* (Thorp), *How to Play Winning Blackjack* (Braun), and *Professional Blackjack* (Wong).

When you play this strategy in conjunction with the High-Low Point Count System, never vary your bet by more than 4 to 1 (e.g., $5 to $20 when playing with a $1000 bankroll). The pit bosses are much more conscious of card counters in single-deck games in Las Vegas and can bar anyone they choose. You should never bet more than one-fiftieth of your total bankroll.

Basic Strategy for Las Vegas Single-Deck Blackjack

Your Hand	Rules for Dealer's Up-cards
8	Double on 5,6. Otherwise hit.
9	Double on 2-6. Otherwise hit.
10	Double on 2-9. Otherwise hit.
11	Always double.
12	Stand on 4-6. Otherwise hit.

13-16	Stand on 2-6. Otherwise hit.
17	Always stand.
A2 thru A5	Double on 4-6. Otherwise hit.
A6	Double on 2-6. Otherwise hit.
A7	Double on 3-6. Stand on 2,7,8,A. Hit on 9,10.
A8	Double on 6. Otherwise stand.
A9	Always stand.
2,2	Split on 3-7. Otherwise hit.
3,3	Split on 4-7. Otherwise hit.
4,4	Treat as 8 above.
5,5	Treat as 10 above.
6,6	Split on 2-6. Otherwise hit.
7,7	Split on 2-7. Stand on 10. Otherwise hit.
8,8	Always split.
9,9	Split on 2-9 except 7. Stand on 7,10,A.
10,10	Always stand.

If the casino allows doubling down after splitting pairs (e.g., the El Cortez), you would add the following pair-split rules to those above:

> Split 2,2 on dealer 2
> Split 3,3 on dealer 2,3
> Split 4,4 on dealer's 4,5 or 6
> Split 6,6 on dealer 7
> Split 7,7 on dealer 8

If the casino allows surrendering, you would modify the above rules and surrender the following hands:

1. Against a dealer ace you would surrender:
   10,6
2. Against a dealer 10 or face card you would surrender:
   9,6; 9,7; 10,5; 10,6; 7,7

The second skill you must develop in order to win at blackjack is card counting. Card counting has been covered at length in Chapter 5, so it will not be discussed in detail here.

Single-deck blackjack is a good game under the right conditions. If you can find a head-to-head game (you alone against the dealer) where the dealer will deal you half a deck before reshuffling, you can gain a nice advantage.

But these games are difficult to find. Single-deck games, because of their popularity, are usually dealt to full tables. If you play at a full table, you will be dealt only two hands in between shuffles. This is not enough hands to exploit the card-counting skills discussed in Chapter 5.

A head-to-head game is much more advantageous because you will be dealt more hands before the shuffle point and therefore more high-count hands where you have an advantage and can increase your bet. You are more apt to find these games in the downtown casinos. I suggest trying the El Cortez, the Golden Gate and the Horseshoe Club, in that order.

At the El Cortez and Golden Gate they deal half a deck before shuffling and at the Horseshoe they deal three hands. The best hours are weekdays about noon when new tables are opening up, during the dinner hour and in the wee hours of the morning. These casinos are not as plush as the Strip hotels, but they offer an atmosphere and people more reminiscent of the old west. Also, your minimum bets are as low as $1, and usually $2. It is difficult to find a $2 single-deck game on the Strip.

SINGLE-DECK BLACKJACK IN RENO/TAHOE CASINOS

In Reno/Tahoe casinos, the rules are not as liberal but this is more than offset by dealing more of the deck before the shuffle. All of the games are single-deck with the exception of the MGM Grand and some of the tables at the Cal-Neva Lodge in Northern Tahoe.

The general Reno/Tahoe rules are:

• double-down permitted only on 10 or 11

• split and resplit any pair

• no surrender

• no double after splitting pairs

• dealer hits soft 17

The basic strategy for these rules is tabulated on the facing page:

Basic Strategy for Reno/Tahoe Single-Deck Blackjack

Your Hand	Rules for Dealer's Up-cards
8	Always hit.
9	Always hit.
10	D 2-9. O/W H
11	Always double.
12	S 4,5,6. O/W H
13,14,15,16	S 2-6. O/W H
17-21	Always stand.
A,2 thru A,6	Always hit.
A,7	S 2-8. O/W H
A,8 thru A,10	Always stand.
A,A	Always split.
2,2	P 3-7. O/W H
3,3	P 4-7. O/W H
4,4	Always hit.
5,5	D 2-9. O/W H
6,6	P 2-6. O/W H
7,7	P 2-7. S 10. O/W H
8,8	Always split.
9,9	P 2-9 X 7. O/W S
10,10	Always stand.

Legend:
D   Double-Down
P   Split Pairs
H   Hit
S   Stand
O/W Otherwise
X   Except

The best casinos to play in Reno are the Nevada Club and Harold's Club. They deal three-fourths of the deck and sometimes deal to the bottom. A head-to-head game can be found in these casinos at similar times to those found in Las Vegas casinos.

At the Sahara and Harrah's, only about half a deck is dealt; you can find a better game at most other casinos. Stay away from the MGM Grand unless you wish to play the four-deck shoe—a very unfavorable game with Reno/Tahoe rules.

The best casinos in the Tahoe area are Harvey's Wagon Wheel at Stateline and the Nevada Club in Northern Tahoe. At Harvey's be a little bit selective about which pit you play in—some of the pit bosses instruct their dealers to deal two hands and shuffle if they suspect you of counting. The Nevada Club in North Tahoe deals a full deck in many cases.

Chapter 13
How to Count Cards in a Single-Deck Game

The reason that so few blackjack players win at single-deck blackjack is that they have difficulty counting in the face-down single-deck game. They get confused as the dealer turns over previously unexposed cards and forget which cards they have counted and which cards they have not counted. I will solve this problem by describing a procedure for counting in the single-deck game.

CARD-COUNTING PROCEDURE
(one-deck: face down)

1. Count the dealer's up-card.
2. Count your two cards.

3. Count the cards taken by each of the other players as they are dealt face up.

4. When a player breaks, count his two cards as he turns them over.

5. When a player doubles-down or splits a pair, count his two cards as he turns them over.

6. Count the dealer's hole-card when he turns it over; count the dealer's drawn cards as he takes them.

7. After the dealer plays his hand he pays off the players who have not broken. Count the players' unexposed *two* cards as they are turned over.

   The dealer will turn these over so they are the two cards closest to him. Do not confuse them with cards previously drawn. Refer to the diagram below:

	10	dealer up-card
	7⎫	
Before the payoff	3⎬	player's drawn cards
	5⎭	
	☐⎫	player unexposed
	☐⎭	cards are 3,2
	10,8	dealer cards
	3⎫	count these two cards
After the payoff	2⎭	as they are turned over
	7	
	3	
	5	

8. It is extremely important that you count the same way every time. Don't be tempted to count your neighbor's cards if you see his hand. This will confuse your procedure at the end of the hand.

CHAPTER 14

HOW TO PLAY
THE LAS VEGAS SHOE GAME

The Las Vegas Shoe Game has been covered in depth in many other blackjack books, therefore a detailed discussion is beyond the scope of this book. But a few comments are in order.

1. Under the right conditions (see Chapter 11), single-deck blackjack is a much more favorable game than the four-deck shoe. The basic strategy advantage in a typical single-deck game is close to even. In the four-deck shoe, the basic strategy advantage is about -0.4 to -0.5% in the better games. To win at the shoe game, this deficit must be eliminated through the betting spread and the method of play.

2. The betting spread should be increased from 4 to 1 to 8 to 1. Select a betting table from Chapter 6. If you are a $5 bettor, you should spread between $5 and $40 ($5 to two hands of $20 on favorable situations) and carry a minimum $2000 bankroll. Cut your bet per hand down by about $5 if you play two hands.

3. Your method of play should be altered to conform to that described in Stanford Wong's *Professional Blackjack*. You should never play at a table where the running count is minus. Learn to move around and sit down only at tables where you see the running count is positive. You can do this either at the beginning or early in the shoe. Glance at the first hands dealt and quickly pick up the running count—if it's +4 or more, sit down. If not, keep walking. When you do sit down and the count turns negative—walk. Why play with the disadvantage of a negative count added to your inherent four-deck disadvantage?

4. If you play the Shoe Game, I recommend the following Las Vegas casinos (basic strategy advantage shown in parentheses):

Caesars   (−0.27%)
MGM   (−0.37%)
Sands   (−0.48%)

BASIC STRATEGY FOR FOUR OR MORE DECKS
(with double-down after split, single-deck and double-deck variations)

The following matrix can be used to tailor a basic strategy to any Nevada shoe, single-deck or double-deck game with the noted rules variations.

Basic Strategy for Four or More Decks

With DDAS and One-Deck Variations

Your Hand	2	3	4	5	6	7	8	9	10	A
5,3	H	H	H	H [D]	H [D]	H	H	H	H	H
6,2	H	H	H	H	H	H	H	H	H	H
9	H [D]	D	D	D	D	H	H	H	H	H
10	D	D	D	D	D	D	D	H	H	H
11	D	D	D	D	D	D	D	D	D	H [D]
10,2	H	H	S [H]	S	S [H]	H	H	H	H	H
Other 12s	H	H	S	S	S	H	H	H	H	H

13	S	S	S	S	S	H	H	H	H	H
14	S	S	S	S	S	H	H	H	H	H
15	S	S	S	S	S	H	H	H	H	H
16	S	S	S	S	S	H	H	H	H	H
17-21	S	S	S	S	S	S	S	S	S	S
A,2	H	H	H[D]	D	D	H	H	H	H	H
A,3	H	H	H[D]	D	D	H	H	H	H	H
A,4	H	H	D	D	D	H	H	H	H	H
A,5	H	H	D	D	D	H	H	H	H	H
A,6	H[D]	D	D	D	D	H	H	H	H	H
A,7	S	D	D	D	D	S	S	H	H	H[S]
A,8	S	S	S	S	S[D]	S	S	S	S	S
A,9	S	S	S	S	S	S	S	S	S	S
A,A	P	P	P	P	P	P	P	P	P	P
2,2	H(P) [P]	P	P	P	P	P	H	H	H	H

3,3	H (P)	H (P)	P	P	P	P	H	H	H	H
4,4	H	H	H*	[D] H (P)	[D] H (P)	H	H	H	H	H
5,5	D	D	D	D	D	D	D	D	H	H
6,6	[P] H (P)	P	P	P	P	H*	H	H	H	H
7,7	P	P	P	P	P	P	H*	H	H [S]	H
8,8	P	P	P	P	P	P	P	P	P	P
9,9	P	P	P	P	P	S	P	P	S	S
10,10	S	S	S	S	S	S	S	S	S	S

CODE: [ ]   One-Deck Variations   *   Split if DDAS and one-deck

(P)   Split if doubling down after splitting allowed—takes precedence over doubling on 4,4 versus 5 and 6

NOTE: If you are playing a two-deck game, the above four-deck strategy should be used with two exceptions:

9—Double on 2-6; otherwise, hit.

11—If 9-2 or 8-3, hit on ace. Otherwise, double.

CHAPTER 15
Tips for Maximizing Your Profits in the Las Vegas Casinos

In this chapter I will discuss the four major variables which the experienced blackjack player must consider when selecting a game in which to play in the Las Vegas casinos. These are: (1) *number of decks,* (2) *blackjack rules,* (3) *decks dealt before shuffling* and, (4) the *betting spread* (the ratio between the minimum bet and the maximum bet, which is used by card counters to take advantage of favorable situations) that one can get away with. I will discuss each of these variables in subsequent paragraphs.

LOOK FOR LIBERAL RULES

It is possible to find single-, double-, four-, five- and six-deck blackjack games offered in various Las Vegas casinos. Most players know that single-deck blackjack is more favorable to the player than the multideck shoe games. One reason is that the player is dealt more blackjacks in a single-deck game. Another is that more high-count opportunities occur. Therefore, the card counter has the advantage a higher percentage of the time and, theoretically, can win more money in the single-deck game.

If you are a basic strategy player and not a card counter, you should definitely seek out and play in the single-deck games. With basic strategy you are essentially playing an even game against the casino.

If you are a card counter, you should forget about the single-deck games and seek out the more profitable double-deck or four-deck games. The reason is that in single-deck games most dealers will deal you only two or three hands at the most before reshuffling. It is very frustrating to the card counter to see a favorable high count (the remaining deck rich in 10-value cards and aces, which provide the player with an advantage) and then see this favorable situation get shuffled away before he or she can take advantage of it. Because of their popularity, most single-deck games are dealt to full tables; even if you should find a head-to-head game, the dealer usually will not deal more than the two or three hands before shuffling up.

Experienced blackjack players are always ready to exploit liberal rules offered by many of the Las Vegas casinos. Some of these are: double-down after pair splitting (e.g., being dealt a pair of 6s, splitting them, drawing a 5 to the first split 6, and doubling the bet on that hand in return for taking only one more card), resplitting pairs (being dealt a pair of 7s, splitting them, drawing a 7 to the first split 7, and splitting that to play a total of three hands each with a separate bet), surrender (throwing in your hand and surrendering half your bet after the dealer has checked for a blackjack, the dealer stands on soft 17 (an ace and one or more cards that total 6). Finding and playing these rules will minimize the casino advantage over the basic strategy player and allow the card counter to maximize his advantage over the casino. On the Las Vegas Strip, the MGM Grand and Caesars Palace offer doubling down after splitting. The El Cortez offers this rule in its downtown location. Most downtown casinos offer resplitting but compensate for this advantage by allowing the dealer to hit instead of stand on soft 17. The Strip casinos all stand on the soft 17. Late surrender is offered at Caesars Palace and the Riviera on the Las Vegas Strip and El Cortez and the Las Vegas Club downtown.

With its single-deck game and favorable rules, El Cortez offers the best game in town to the basic strategy player. Card counters should stay away from the El Cortez, however, for reasons I will discuss later in this chapter.

The Las Vegas Club, downtown, offers the most liberal rules but deals a six-deck game. In addition to the liberal rules discussed above, they allow you to double-down on three- or four-card hands, draw more than one card to split aces, and get paid automatically for six-card hands.

HOW TO SET UP AN EARLY SURRENDER DECISION

I had a very interesting experience with an early surrender decision on this trip to Las Vegas. A certain Strip casino was offering surrender but didn't understand the difference between early surrender and late surrender. (Early surrender is when you can surrender before the dealer checks for blackjacks—a much more advantageous decision; late surrender is when you may surrender your hand and lose half your bet after the dealer checks for blackjack. Of course, if the dealer has blackjack with late surrender you don't get to surrender your hand as you do with early surrender.) One of my instructors was playing the hand and showed a 14 against an ace—a normal surrender on the early surrender basic strategy. He asked the dealer if he could surrender before she peeked to determine whether or not she had blackjack. She said no. So my instructor called the pit boss over and asked him if he could surrender his hand before the dealer checked for blackjack any time the dealer showed an ace or a 10-value card. The pit boss said sure, let him surrender any time he wants. The dealer then made the comment that the house would not offer surrender if it were not to their advantage. My instructor and I enjoyed a very nice early surrender advantage in a double-deck blackjack game for the remainder of our stay.

GETTING BARRED AT THE EL CORTEZ

I have only been barred from four casinos in my entire professional blackjack career. One of them is the El Cortez in downtown Las Vegas. I have been barred a number of times at the El Cortez. In fact, they bar me every time I play there. No, they don't recognize me, but yes, they do bar any card counter who tries to "take advantage of them" by employing a 4 to 1 or more betting spread.

The first time they barred me was in 1977 when I was doing research for *Blackjack: A Winner's Handbook*. I was betting from $5 to $20 and beat them for over a thousand dollars in about five days of play. Now that I show them green action ($25 chips), it doesn't take me nearly so long to get barred. On this last trip, it took exactly ten minutes. Here is the story of the latest barring. (I go to the El Cortez just for fun; I know they are going to bar me but I enjoy kidding the pit bosses about it. The El Cortez doesn't send pictures or descriptions of card counters around to the other casinos.)

I bought in for $300—twelve quarter chips—and began playing a quarter a hand. Immediately two pit bosses began watching my play. This is called "heat" in card-counter jargon. El Cortez management suspects anybody betting quarters of being a card counter. The dealer was shuffling after every second hand, so I was not getting a very favorable game.

I began betting $50 on the first hand after the shuffle. If the count was neutral or negative, I would bet $25 on the second hand dealt. I was waiting for a favorable situation—a count of +3 or higher in this single-deck game to make a $100 bet. Even though I was not getting the favorable situation, I got lucky and quickly won about $375 after five minutes of play. The heat became more intense. I tried to make eye contact with the two pit bosses but to no avail. They were waiting for their opportunity to pounce.

They finally got it. The count shot up to +6 after the first hand was dealt. A very favorable situation for me, with about a 3% advantage over the casino. I pushed out four green chips and the young pit boss walked over. This time they didn't bar me; they merely shuffled away my 3% advantage and restored the deck to a neutral situation. I grabbed my $100 from the betting circle, looked the pit boss in the eye and said, "What's the matter, can't you guys stand a measly four to one betting spread? There is no way I can make any money here with the kind of game that you're dealing."

"We know you're a card counter," he said. "We won't even let you raise your bet by a dime." After a few more good-natured barbs, I got into pretty good communication with this pit boss. He told me that since the casino was so small, they just couldn't afford to allow any card counter, no matter how small he or she is betting, to take a shot at their very modest bankroll. Oh well, I'll try them again next year.

BUYING A 50 TO 1 BETTING SPREAD

Most of the card counter's advantage at the game of blackjack is derived by maximizing his betting spread. He must know how much to bet according to the count, his bankroll, the degree of risk he is willing to take and the number of decks remaining to be played. The reason that so few card counters win money at blackjack is because they just don't know how to balance these four variables. I would love to deal a blackjack game to all the card counters barred from Atlantic City casinos. Most of them know how to count okay, but they bet too much in proportion to their bankroll or take too high a degree of risk and end up going broke. I wish casino managers understood the mathematics of the game of blackjack, especially in the area of money management.

I am going to show you how I achieved a 50 to 1 betting spread in a Las Vegas casino, but I don't recommend your trying this unless you have the proper bankroll to back it up. The Las Vegas Strip casino where this happened allows a minimum bet of $2 and a maximum bet of $100. I began play by buying $300 worth of quarter chips. My plan was to bet from $25 to $100 depending upon the count.

In the first half of the double-deck game the count stayed in the neutral-to-slightly negative range, so I was betting a flat $25. With a little more than one deck remaining, the count jumped to +5, so I bet $50. I won. The count was now +7—a very favorable betting opportunity. I bet $100. The dealer, with absolutely no heat of any kind from the pit, decided to shuffle up. My favorable opportunity was lost as the deck was shuffled to a neutral state.

I decided to try a different strategy on this particular dealer. I wanted to see just how much I could get away with so I could pass this information on to my students taking a summer blackjack class from me in the Los Angeles area. After the shuffle, I bet $2. I kept betting $2 as long as the count was negative. When the count turned positive, I began to progress my bet upward depending on the count and the number of remaining decks. I didn't have to worry about the bankroll size or risk factors because my bankroll could support a much larger bet than the $100 maximum offered by the casino.

The count kept getting higher and my bet progressed to $25. Now, the count was +6 again with about one deck remaining to be played. The same situation in which the dealer had shuffled up on me in the last two decks that were dealt. I made a $50 bet with a $5 bet for the dealer. *We* won the hand. On the next hand the count was still higher. I bet $100 for me and $5 for the dealer. Blackjack! We won again. Since there were three other players in the game, only about a quarter deck remained to be dealt. I bet another $100 with a $5 bet for the dealer. No shuffle. He dealt out another winning hand. By this time there were only a few cards left to be played so he had no choice but to shuffle up.

After about an hour of this "friendly collaboration" I picked up my stacks of green chips, the dealer and I gave each other a knowing smile and I left the casino. A little bribery will go a long way.

MAXIMIZE YOUR BETTING SPREAD AGAINST INEXPERIENCED DEALERS

As discussed above, the betting spread is the single most important variable to the card counter. Used properly, it maximizes the counter's winning advantage. I currently enjoy a betting spread of 20 to 1 in the Atlantic City casinos, which gives me a healthy winning edge. On the other hand, the betting spread can also be disastrous to a counter who overbets his or her bankroll. Many counters believe that they are invincible when the count is very high, e.g., 10 to 15 with three or fewer decks remaining in the six-deck Atlantic City game. Without knowing it, they increase their risk factor (the mathematical probability of losing their entire bankroll) and overbet their hand. If they lose they wonder what happened and begin chasing their money like any common gambler. *Sizing one's bet and discipline in money management are the keys to winning at blackjack.* As mentioned above, a card counter must consider not only the count, but his bankroll, his risk factor and the number of remaining decks in computing an optimum bet size.

On my trip to Las Vegas last summer, I was able to accomplish a 75 to 1 betting spread at the Jolly Trolley. The Jolly Trolley is a very small casino sitting at the downtown edge of the Strip as part of a small, noisy shopping center. They offer double-deck and four-deck blackjack games with a minimum bet of $1 and a maximum bet of $25. Normally I would not play in a casino offering such a low maximum bet, but I was doing some research for students attending my summer BLACK-JACK CLINIC in the Los Angeles area.

Naturally I chose a double-deck game because of the smaller casino-advantage when measured against the basic strategy plays. I began by playing $1 per hand because my objective was to maximize my betting spread without getting kicked out. For the first half hour of play the count remained in a slightly negative, to neutral, to slightly positive range. Consequently, my bet did not surpass the $10 level. On a couple of hands I bet $10 on each of two hands with no heat whatsoever—an easy $1 to $20 or 20 to 1 betting spread.

All of a sudden the count shot up. With about a deck and a half left to play, I bet $25 on one hand. Now, the pit boss was showing me some attention. A rather young and friendly fellow, he came over and eyeballed my stack of chips: a mixture of fives, ones and even fifty-cent pieces. He wasn't so concerned about the size of my bet as he was about the chip mixture. He had the dealer break the stack down and put out five $5 chips. I lost this hand but as the count was still very high, I decided to bet two hands of $25 each. Having a lot of $5 and $1 chips in front of me, I again put out two tall stacks, mostly of $1 chips. The pit boss wandered over again and with the usual paranoia of card counters, I thought he was going to bar me for sure. After all, I had bet $1 in this same two-deck deal and was now making a $50 bet, for an almost unheard-of betting spread of 50 to 1. (In most Las Vegas casinos in a double-deck game, a 6 to 1 or an 8 to 1 betting spread is the most you can get away with without being shuffled up on or being asked to leave the premises.) Again, the pit boss was more interested in the size and content of my bet than in my betting spread, which he had failed to notice. He had the dealer break down a few stacks and put up two stacks of five $5 chips each. Because of the low betting maximum—$25—this particular table had no $25 chips.

I won this hand and, as the count was still high, I

decided to "go for the throat." I bet three hands of $25 each (a 75 to 1 spread). No problem, no heat. The dealer did not even call the bet out to the pit box. I won two out of three of these hands, played a few more hands at $75 each and had to ask for a rack to carry my many $5 chips to the cashier's cage.

There are many casinos like the Jolly Trolley in Las Vegas, and if you are a small- to medium-range bettor, you should definitely seek them out to maximize your winning advantage. The Jolly Trolley had just recently reopened and was just not concerned with card counters. The dealers were all green, very inexperienced, and required most of the attention of the pit personnel.

TAKE ADVANTAGE OF DECK PENETRATION

With the exception of one or two double-deck games, the Las Vegas four-deck shoe game offers the most favorable advantage to the card counter. The major reason is deck penetration. The farther into the deck the dealer deals before shuffling, the greater the card counter's advantage. In most Las Vegas Strip games about one deck is cut off from the end to mark the shuffle point. If you scout around, however, you can find some games where one-half or even less is cut off from the end—3½ decks or more are dealt! The result is more hands are dealt when the count is high and more money is won on these favorable high-count betting opportunities. And that, after all, is what the game is all about.

CHAPTER 16
Blackjack Trip to Reno/Tahoe

Last spring, when my exposure index (pit boss attention units divided by hours of playing time) in the A.C. casinos was getting a little too high, I decided it was time to leave town for a while and give my many A.C. "friends" a chance to forget about me. Where to go was an easy decision to make—Lake Tahoe, Nevada. Some of the best skiing in the world, coupled with the best single-deck blackjack games in the world. The perfect vacation—shussing down the slopes during the day and slaying the dealers at night.

I informed Nancy, who is always ready to go on any blackjack trip, we packed our bags and departed the following Sunday for our condo in Incline Village, Nevada—right in the middle of ski and casino country and only an hour's drive from Reno.

As I was a little rusty on my single-deck numbers (true count or index numbers deciding when to depart from basic strategy), I packed my dog-eared copy of Stanford Wong's *Professional Blackjack,* together with the usual stop watch, practice decks, fresh cards and most recent copies of Wong's *Blackjack Newsletter,* to inform me of where the best games are. Little did I realize that this newsletter would lead me to the best blackjack game in the world. Yes, even better than our friendly Atlantic City games.

Reno/Tahoe casino blackjack differs greatly from the Las Vegas games in the south. First of all, with one or two exceptions, all of the games are single-deck. Secondly, the rules of play are much more stringent than in the Las Vegas casinos. For example, you may double-down only on 10 or 11, you may not double-down after splitting pairs and, with one exception, there is no surrender. But the game is still a very good one, in fact better than the Las Vegas games because many of the Reno/Tahoe casinos will deal you two-thirds or more of a deck before reshuffling. This fact provides the counter with a very nice advantage—greater than 1.5%. Here is the strategy that I used for playing the Reno/Tahoe blackjack tables: (1) Play a single-deck basic strategy with variations as described in Wong's *Professional Blackjack;* (2) Play a 1 to 4 betting spread. I bet $25 on any negative count, $50 if the true count (the true count is equal to the running count divided by the remaining decks or fraction thereof) is 1, and $75 to $100 if the true count is 2 or more. I planned to progress from $25 to $100 in steps. Otherwise I would arouse the suspicions of the dealer or the pit boss, who then might ask the dealer to shuffle the deck. Remember, in a one-deck game, it is much easier to shuffle than it is to break a four- or six-deck shoe; (3) I also planned to move around from pit to pit and from casino to casino. Betting $25 to $100 quickly arouses the attention of the floorpersons and pit bosses. They are much more conscious of card counters in Nevada, probably because there are no restrictions on tossing them out of the casino. I would not play more than a half an hour at any one table and more than one to two hours in any one casino; (4) In North Tahoe, my selected casino was the Nevada Club because they deal you more of the deck than they do at the other casinos. In South Tahoe, I chose Harvey's Wagon Wheel for the same reason. In Reno, my play was mainly confined to Harold's Club, the Nevada Club and the Bonanza. The Bonanza is a very interesting little casino that offered, at that time, the best blackjack game in the world. The casino was identified in the March 1980 issue of Stanford Wong's *Blackjack Newsletter* (Pi Yee Press, Box 1144, La Jolla, CA 92038). I mention the newsletter to acknowledge it as being a tremendous source of information about casino playing conditions for experienced blackjack players playing in more than one location. This particular piece of information was worth, to me, much more than the cost of my skiing/casino holiday in the Reno/Tahoe area.

After a few days of skiing and playing the Tahoe casinos successfully, I was ready to take on the Reno casinos and, in particular, the Bonanza. It is on the outskirts of town, in an innocuous-looking little shopping center. It has a railing around the front with a wooden walkway, reminiscent of the Old West. I almost expected to see a few horses tied at the front door and some cowboys with six-shooters standing around on the inside. The casino is very small. It offers six blackjack tables and perhaps one to two hundred slot machines and that's it— no craps or roulette. The rules are the best: a single-deck game, early surrender, double-down only on 10 or 11, etc., the same as the other Reno/Tahoe casinos. These favorable rules, especially early surrender, gave me an edge of 0.1% right off the top. But the best thing about this game was the fact that they dealt 50 out of the 52 cards. They burned the first card (moved it right to the discard tray) and did not deal the last card. There is no other place in the world, to my knowledge, where a full deck is dealt to the player. The advantages of such a game are enormous. At one point, I had a running count of 6 (computed with the High-Low point count: 2-6 count as + 1; 7-9 count as zero; 10, J, Q, K, A count as − 1) with six cards remaining to be played. I knew, of course, that I would get a 10 or an ace. It is nice to pick up your first card and see exactly what you knew you would get.

That first morning I was betting modestly, feeling the place out, and determining just how much I could get away with. I was betting $10 to $40, depending on the count. The cards were running just so-so, and about noontime I was down about $150. I took a break for lunch, after converting my $5 chips to $25 chips. After returning from lunch, I announced in a voice loud enough for the single pit boss to hear that I had to pick up my wife and kids from the slopes and that it was time to bet up and get even. I stepped up my bets to $25 and $100 and began to get serious. There was one other exciting feature about this game. I was the only player. I had a head-to-head game with 50 cards being dealt to me. What else can a blackjack player ask for? Since there were not that many $25 players visiting this little casino, there was only one row of quarter chips (blackjack jargon for $25 chips) in the rack. I quickly cleaned that out. The pit boss nicely brought over some additional quarter chips. I quickly cleaned out the quarter chips the second time. The scene was repeated a third time. The pit boss was paying absolutely no attention to me, I was getting a nice run of cards, and the $25 to $100 betting range depending on the true count was working out just fine ($100 was the maximum bet allowed).

Now, it was time to make a graceful exit and return to Tahoe to pick up the wife and kids. By this time there were four to five mountains of green chips in front of me. Normally I would have put them in my pocket and tried to hide them, but because I was the only green-chips player in the casino and they knew exactly how many green chips they had filled the rack with and how many I had won, there was no reason to hide the chips. I asked the pit boss for a rack and he kindly brought me one immediately. I packed the rack with my chips and walked over to the cashier's window. I cashed in about $2150 in chips, which caused the cashier a minor problem. I cleaned out her seven $100 bills and two $50s, so the remainder was paid in $20s, $10s and $5s. She was complaining in a good-natured way about my taking all her cash. In the meantime, my pocket was bulging with bills. What to do? Do I walk out the door? Or do I look like a casual gambler and go over to the bar for some good-natured conversation and a drink? I chose the latter course of action, walked to the bar, ordered a scotch and water, and was pleasantly surprised when the pit boss paid for the drink. I chatted with the bartenders for a while about skiing, thanked the pit boss on the way out, told him I had had a fantastic run of cards, and that I would see him again in a couple of days after getting in a little more skiing. He invited me back. Fantastic.

The same scene was repeated the next day. The only difference this time was that I had two or three more players with me at the table. So, I was playing two hands of $25 and $100 per hand. When lunchtime came, I was $1300 ahead and had to call for another rack. The pit boss graciously brought one over. After I had cashed in and cleaned out all of the cashier's large bills again, the pit boss offered to buy me lunch. I accepted, and enjoyed a nice lunch on the house and then returned to the tables for further play. I played for another couple of hours, breaking even, and then made a very graceful exit.

Unfortunately I didn't do much skiing for the remainder of our stay. Squaw Valley, Heavenly Valley and North Star would have to wait. I've never had a problem with keeping my priorities straight. Also, Harold's Club and the Nevada Club would have the good fortune of not seeing much of me during this skiing/casino holiday.

The Bonanza was in. Most of my waking hours were spent there. My wife did not let me stay over in Reno, so I had to waste time commuting back and forth each day. A very expensive commute in terms of additional monies not won.

But wait. Before you pack your bags and head for Reno

and the Bonanza, I have some bad news for you. The rules were changed. About a month after I left, early surrender was eliminated and they began shuffling at the half- to three-quarter-deck mark.

But there is good news. I was talking to Wong last night. Another Reno casino has changed its rules—a 0.25% edge is possible right off the top. Throw in your counting system and you have close to a 2% advantage. Which one? I can't tell you. Not until I get out there and get my share first. (Editor's Note: You'll find the name of this casino in the December 1980 issue of Stanford Wong's *Current Blackjack News*, Pi Yee Press, Box 1144, La Jolla, CA 92038.)

SECTION V

Blackjack in the Caribbean

Section Overview

Chapter 17 contains correspondence between me and a BLACKJACK CORRESPONDENCE COURSE student living in Curaçao, Netherlands, Antilles. The correspondence yields a keen insight into the development of an advanced blackjack player, while providing details on the conduct of blackjack games in Curaçao, Aruba and the Dominican Republic. Chapters 18, 19 and 20 describe blackjack adventures in the Bahamas and Puerto Rico.

Chapter 17

Blackjack
in Curaçao and Aruba

INTRODUCTION

The correspondence below is excerpted from letters from a BLACKJACK CORRESPONDENCE COURSE student in Curaçao. My answers to his questions and my comments on his writings are interspaced, where necessary, to make the chapter logically cohesive. To protect the privacy of this student, who is today playing semiprofessional blackjack, I give him the fictitious initials of K. B.

Curaçao, November 29, 1978

Dear Mr. Patterson:

I live in Curaçao and work here as a teacher of English on a three-year contract basis.

As you will probably know they have got four casinos here, just as in Aruba, and it is just about the only entertainment so I decided to take blackjack up seriously. I have been a consistent loser at the roulette table which I discovered in Suriname where I also worked three years. Back in Holland, playing in Austria, Belgium and England, I did not do so badly but the American roulette is killing all the systems (the zero and double zero).

During my vacation last summer in Las Vegas, I met Howard Grossman, who teaches blackjack. Unfortunately I was already broke but at the Gambler's Book Club, I bought *Beat the Dealer, Playing Blackjack as a Business* and your book. I have studied pretty seriously and can now play basic strategy perfectly. Last week in Aruba I won $100 for the first time playing against the blackjack machines.

From the above you will have gathered that I would like to be an advanced blackjack player to add to my meager teacher's salary. Over here they have four decks and the rules are doubling down only on 10-11. I could also play in Puerto Rico if I am "advanced" enough. I would like to buy your self-instruction course or do you agree with Howard Grossman that at home you simply cannot learn it properly?

I am also in need of the books recommended by you viz: *21 Counting Methods to Beat 21*, Humble, L., *Blackjack Gold* and Wong, S., *Professional Blackjack.*

I will be most grateful if you could help me and will send you a cheque as soon as I know what this will cost me.

Hoping to hear from you soon,

I remain,

K. B.

Curaçao, December 28, 1978

Dear Jerry:

I was pleased to receive your answer and so as not to waste any more time I would like to start immediately with your course.

I hope I am not a nuisance but I have some questions.

1. If you play basic strategy is it better to stand on 16 versus 10 if your 16 consists of three cards?

Answer: No.

2. If you can't soft-double-down should you stand on A,6 versus 2,8?

Answer: No. Always hit this hand.

3. In a four-deck game should I double-down on 6,2 (8) versus 5 or 6?

Answer: No. Hit this hand.

4. If you play basic strategy perfectly wouldn't a good betting system give you an advantage, e.g., D'Alembert or Ascot? From experience I know they don't work for roulette but there the odds are against you and this is not the case with blackjack.

Answer: No. You must count cards in order to gain an advantage at blackjack.

Last but not least, I wish you a Happy New Year and hope that you can really turn me into a winner.

All the Best,

K. B.

Curaçao, January 18, 1979

Dear Jerry:

Thank you for your letter with the good advice which came too late, unfortunately. As you requested, here are the rules for the Curaçao casinos:

1. All games are four decks.

2. Rules vary. In three casinos, Plaza—Hilton—Holiday Inn (now Holiday Beach Hotel): doubling down only on 10 and 11. In Plaza—Hilton (same management) they burn only one card. In the Hilton they show the burn-card. Hitting soft 17: some do, some don't. In Holiday Beach Hotel they burn five cards! These three casinos: *no* hole-card.

3. In the Princess Isle Hotel, you can double-down on 8,9,10,11 and soft-doubling down is allowed. They do take a hole-card. They deal, however, only half a four-deck shoe.

4. All pair-splitting allowed. However, if you get a third pair it differs (in Aruba I was allowed to split a third 8).

5. Insurance: Yes, all. Surrender: none.

6. Only one casino has a hole-card, which is checked after each player has been dealt two cards.

7. I don't know whether they bar counters who are spotted. Actually, I have tried to spot counters but so far have only seen losers.

Last but not least, Jerry, your advice about not playing for the time being I will strictly adhere to as I have been losing about $500 lately. In the meantime, my blackjack history is: Aruba: three wins of $30 against the machine; about $25 win at the Concorde. In Curaçao I kept winning small amounts to a total of $250. This I lost all in one evening at the Princess Isle (with the unfavorable rules). My betting method was $5 and then you know the 2,3,4,5,6,7.* The minimum is $3. In a few hours I kept

---

*A system I used in roulette: you start in the middle (5) and if you win you bet 6; if you lose, you bet 4, etc., until you either reach 3 or 7.

losing and after that, apart from minor wins of $15 and $45, I have been consistently losing.

I have played basic strategy for four decks as outlined in your book and Revere, and I am 100% sure I played it perfectly. Meanwhile I received Koko Ita's book, Wong's book and *Blackjack Gold*. The latter book stresses the cheating and, to tell the truth, I also have the feeling that in the Princess Isle Hotel there are too few dealer busts. I thought counting was impossible until I read *21 Counting Methods* by Koko Ita. The problem now is to find a belt or gadget to count.

Right now my action item is practicing the Wong-approach combined with the betting system as outlined by Koko Ita. I am enthusiastic that it works, at home at least. It is possible to find a head-on game here, but only at the $5-minimum table. There are only one or two $3-minimum (at the Hilton they have a $2 minimum but expert dealers). At the Holiday Beach Hotel some dealers supposedly split profits with certain locals and I suspect them of cheating. At the Princess Isle Hotel they have lady dealers under 30 (according to Humble, ideal), but I don't trust them (only half a four-deck, few dealer busts).

As soon as I am ready I think I'll concentrate on Aruba for weekends. Humble gives Aruba a very good rating and I agree, also the casinos are much bigger.

Sorry to have been so long-winded, but I thought I'd better write you all that crops up in my mind. Hopefully you won't find it too chaotic.

Right now I am about $500 down and I promise I won't play until you say I am ready.

Yours truly,

K. B.

Curaçao, April 29, 1979

Dear Jerry:

I have just come back from the Dominican Republic and have been playing quite a bit.

First of all, the result is a loss of $270—I was staying at the Jarigua Hotel and the dealers are extremely fast (one of them was dealing like a whirlwind, many of them were so fast you didn't get the time to double, etc.). Playing conditions (rules) are all right—doubling down allowed on any number + DDAS (I found that out later, on the last day to be exact). In another casino, NACO, they have even better rules: there they also have surrender. If you have five cards, you can opt for payment of half your bet and with a dealer's 10 showing you can insure. (I've never seen that before and it is paid 7-2, I believe.) Then there is El Embajador: a place to avoid; run by a Chinese; here they burn four cards.

Before the last day I was $200 up and then quickly lost $100 in El Embajador, and then I played for a considerable time in Jarigua and was steadily losing. I could only very roughly keep the count. I also had a similar experience as you have mentioned. I was dealt two 8s versus a dealer's 10. I had $30 staked, so after splitting, I had $60 on the table. I was dealt a 10 on my first 8 and another 8 on my second, which I split again. Anyway, instead of winning $90, I lost $90 because the dealer turned up a nice "twenty."

All in all, it was a good experience, because I find now that I can very easily keep the count here now (the dealers are slow-coaches here in Curaçao).

Now I have a number of questions which are also partly observations, experiences, feelings, etc.

1. In my home-sessions, I can't get any profit with the Wong-approach. I am down $800, using the Wong-System and betting according to the running count. After about 900 hands it is very frustrating!

2. I agree with you, Wong is comparatively easy to memorize, but his numbers refer to the true count and that is very hard to calculate in practice. In Revere's book, page 137, he gives a beautiful chart to calculate the true count. Also when to take insurance—Wong says 2,8! That's a horrible figure! Many of Wong's figures are situations as to be so far-fetched that they are almost nonexistent, e.g., hard doubling down with 10 versus 10 or ace with +4 (true count)! Or his standing on 16 versus 9 on 5 (true count)!

3. The Revere plus-minus strategy is much easier and clearer. For strategy variations, he usually has S H (stand if the count is plus one or more, otherwise hit). This may be less accurate but is easier to apply in casino environments.

In your book you state, page 77, that with a simple point-count system in a four-deck game, you play essentially an even game. Do you still believe this?

4. In home sessions with Revere's Point-Count strategy, I easily build up a profit.

5. I feel attracted to Revere's betting advice. Play until you have won or lost 30 units or until one hour has passed. Over here you can only get a seat at $5 dollar table so this would limit losses to $150. I want your advice as I think I could apply this with a betting-range of $5-$10-$25-$50 and then look upon it as a sort of tennis game, e.g., I want to win six sets and will inevitably lose four sets leaving me with $150 profit on the average. The

advantage is I don't have to carry more than about $300.
Please tell me what you think of this.

6. Wouldn't you say that +2 true count is easier to apply for insurance decisions?

7. In Aruba and Curaçao, you have four decks (−0.52), no double on 9 (−0.14), no soft double (−0.14), hit soft 17 (−0.19), no further pair-splitting (−0.05), no hole-card (−0.13) = −1.18. Even with card-counting, isn't the advantage negligible?

This more or less sums up my "problems." It is not meant as attack on Wong or you, but I've tried to be honest as to my feelings.

Does card counting work when 4 or 5 cards are "burnt" or if only half a four deck is dealt? Revere mentions he would still win with eleven cards burnt (page 93).

Sincerely,

K. B.

MY RESPONSE

May 11, 1979

Dear K. B.:

I don't understand the fact that you are losing at home with the Wong System. I have graduated over 100 students from my Blackjack Clinic and over 90 percent are winning—those that aren't winning are either deviating from the system or overbetting. Two of those that aren't winning just had a series of losing sessions. But they didn't lose their entire bankroll.

Would you mind playing 500 more hands with the following betting method and let me know the results? Start with 500 units of capital.

Running Count	Bet Size (Units)
Minus	2
0-4	3
5-6	5
7-9	8
10 and above	10

1. It is statistically possible that you might have had a bad run of cards and your $800 loss could be a "statistical aberration."

2. Wong's true count numbers do occur. I have split 10s six times in my last 50 hours of play. Of the twelve hands, I lost only one. The others occur often enough to warrant learning if you're a serious blackjack player: see enclosed Lesson 4—you should memorize the -1 to $+6$ range.

3. The Revere plus-minus strategy does, of course, assign the same value to the cards as does Wong's. But Wong's is more accurate and the enclosed Lesson 4 should prepare you to utilize it in a casino.

The comment you refer to on page 77 of my book is true—for the occasional player. Serious students of the game can derive a small advantage by:

• adopting the proper betting spread,

• playing two hands in profitable situations,

- playing true count and varying the basic strategy,

- knowing when to surrender.

4. You say in your home sessions with Revere's plus-minus, you have easily built up a profit, but yet the Revere system and the Wong system are exactly the same except for their use of the true count.

You must be betting differently. Let me answer it further under Question 5.

5. If you carry $300 and then bet $5-10-25-50, you have an excellent chance of getting wiped out! I don't recommend it. Is this the betting strategy you use in home sessions with Revere? If so, you have probably had a run of good luck.

6. Use +3 true count to make your insurance decisions. +2 is inaccurate.

7. Yes, you do have a negligible advantage in Aruba. To overcome it you need a bet variation of at least 8 to 1 and you must play two hands in all favorable situations, i.e., true count = +2 or more.

Best Regards,

Jerry L. Patterson

P.S. K. B., I can make you into a winner but you have to follow my program. If you decide to use Revere, you shouldn't spend any more money with me. I'll understand if you decide to cancel but you should follow through on one program. Stanford Wong I know personally—he has played professionally since 1975 and earns an excellent living using the same High-Low Point Count I'm teaching you. Let me hear from you.

J. P.

Curaçao, May 27, 1979

Dear Jerry,

Thank you very much for your letter and I am glad to be able to say I am doing very well indeed now. I have recovered my $270 loss of Santo Domingo and am now with a modest profit. Especially at the Hilton, I am doing fine (five times a winner, never lost there).

I am pleased to tell you that I am gradually becoming more and more "certain" and during a long weekend in Aruba, I broke even. In spite of your warning, I tried the blackjack machines again after losing the first night about $50, won the second day $100 but realize the danger.

In Holiday Inn—Aruba, they offer surrender after the first two cards (dealer has no hole-card). [J. P. comment: This is a very favorable rule as discussed in the Atlantic City section of this book.]

During the summer vacation, I'll go to Colombia, Brazil, Suriname and Venezuela. In Medellin I plan to play and also in Suriname. Unfortunately, the other countries don't have casinos. If I have a week left (or more), I'd like to go to Puerto Rico and/or St. Martin's. The only thing is that I don't know anything about playing conditions in Puerto Rico. Do you? I only know they have two decks and I read somewhere that gambling in P.R. is for masochists!

I am already looking forward to next year. Then my contract here ends and I intend to go back to Holland via Central America and Mexico and want to see how I'll be doing in Las Vegas. I want to stay there at least a month and then hope to go back via Southeast Asia.

To wind up a few questions:

1. Over here when you have blackjack and the dealer has an ace, you have three possibilities: a) even money; b) you gamble and possibly have "a push"; c) you gamble and insure.

Is there a specific strategy for each occasion?

2. I would also like to play at the Holiday Beach where they burn five cards. If they deal three-fourths of the four-deck shoe, I assume counting still works. Is this correct?

3. In the Princess Isle Hotel (PIH), where they have a hole-card and doubling down is allowed on anything, they "rush" me for the insurance. Should I refrain from using it altogether there?

4. In a head-on game you get three cards for counting (your two + dealer's up-card). Wouldn't it be useful to practice three-card combinations?

Thank you for your excellent course and hope to hear from you soon.

Kind regards,

K. B.

MY RESPONSE

June 9, 1979

Dear K. B.:

Your essay and quiz received with your letter of May

27th show that you understand the importance of money management.

Here are the answers to your questions and concerns:

1. San Juan has very poor rules. I advise you not to play there until you become an advanced blackjack player.

2. Insure in a four-deck game if the true count is 2.8 (you can round to 3.0) or higher.

3. Counting still works even though they burn five cards.

4. You should refrain from insuring at the PIH if you are unsure of the true count. Only buy insurance if it's 3.0 or higher—if you are uncertain, never take insurance.

5. Yes, the three-card combinations would be a good drill. This is an excellent recommendation and I plan to incorporate it into the Correspondence Course.

6. With respect to carrying your bankroll with you, I share your concern. For now you should stick to $5-$20 bets. I would not advise betting more until after you finish Lesson 5—Advanced Money Management.

Looking forward to receiving your completed Lesson 4.

Best Regards,

Jerry L. Patterson

Curaçao, August 10, 1979

Dear Jerry,

First of all I am happy to say I am doing fine. During my holiday in Colombia I did not play much. First I played only one night in Medellin—(Colombia) at the Nutibara Hotel and won about $40—everything is done in a very "amateur-like" way; later in Bogota I lost $80 but it was my own fault as I was having fun with friends I happened to see who could play blackjack in Bogota. I saw a curious play in which they deal a four-deck game right to the end, but unfortunately I was not in good shape. In Brazil there are no casinos. In Suriname, I won about $300. There are only two casinos there—at the Palace Hotel (extremely unfavorable rules: doubling down only on 11) and at the Torarica Hotel (the usual rules) very nice to play in, but you have to be early or every seat is taken.

Now I come to some questions as I find that I'm still learning although I leave the casino a winner three out of four times and my $250 investment in your course promises to be the best bet in life.

1. In Colombia, Suriname and the Antilles, the local people often blame you when they lose and say it is because you're hitting soft 17. When the table is filled up they say if you don't hit, the dealer will bust more frequently (one of them went so far as to say the game is called: "do not hit"). I know it is a myth, but it is very vexing at times.

2. Just before going on a holiday, I found out my basic strategy needs adjusting. Please correct me if I'm wrong.

When the dealer takes no hole-card (Wong, page 124).
Hard 11 versus 10: do not double, hit.
Hard 11 versus A: never double, hit.
Hard 10 versus 10 or A: never double, hit.
A,A versus 10 or A: do not split.

Answer: Correct, except you do split aces against a 10.

3. You said San Juan has poor rules (e.g., double-down on 11 only; four-deck game). I quite agree but over here the rules are just as bad and I keep winning. Isn't it so that good counting and betting possibilities make up for bad rules?

Answer: Yes.

For my own purpose I've been up $1300, then playing better I still started losing until my profits dropped to $300. Since then I've recovered to $700.

I now feel certain to play the system correctly and intend to use the following table: (1) minus: $5; (2) + 1: $10; (3) + 2: $15 etc., up to + 7: $40; (+ 8, + 9 also $40). The reason is I'm now ready to make some real money (bankroll is now $2000).

Last but not least, Jerry, I am very grateful to you. I can easily make as much playing blackjack as I do with teaching.

All the best with kind regards,

K. B.

October 16, 1979

Dear Jerry:

Right now I'm ready to go to Aruba as obviously I don't want to be seen too often in the casinos over here (Curaçao); I've already written down quiz questions on how I have been doing. Funny thing is that in one casino, Plaza (bad rules: no hole, only doubling down on 10-11, no resplitting), I'm up $1100; whereas in the other three I'm slightly down. I don't want to draw any conclusions yet because I play mostly at the Plaza. The one casino where I'm really down, Holiday Beach *(surrender rule*—5 cards burnt—no hole—no resplitting—"bee cards")*, does not offer (as yet) its favorable returns.

This again leads me to the question that if the counting and betting situation is good, bad rules apparently do not affect your profits. In short, the rules are just as bad as in Puerto Rico but I win "pretty nicely" at the Plaza.

Plaza:	*Played:* 44 times: +	$1460
Hilton:	*Played:* 21 times: +	345
Holiday Beach:	*Played:* 29 times: +	105
Princess Isle Hotel:	*Played:* 14 times: −	800
	+	$1110

Conclusion: Plaza and Hilton have the same unfavorable rules. Practically always I play at full tables in all four casinos. However, in the Plaza and Hilton, they deal about three decks! Holiday Beach has the surrender rule. However, they burn five cards and don't allow you to surrender on a $5 bet ($10 and higher). Princess Isle Hotel has Las Vegas rules; however, surprisingly, my worst result also my highest profit $335 and highest loss $420: they deal slightly more than two decks.

On the whole I think that my bad results at the PIH may be due to the wild fluctuations, but Mr. Humble would probably think that he had been cheated.

Please, comment on these results. Keeping in mind that I've always played conservatively, not drawing any attention, it's not too bad. On the other hand, it is not exactly professional blackjack.

Best Regards,
K. B.

Curaçao, January 16, 1980

Dear Jerry,

First of all, I'd like to wish you a happy New Year and express my sincere gratitude toward you for having shown me a profitable way to play blackjack.

Being a teacher and at the same time, of a roving, adventurous disposition, I've tried many things in my life, mostly to end up as in the Rime of the Ancient Mariner: "he rose the following morn, a wiser and a sadder man." I remember the time when I invested $4000 in a video set to be placed in a disco, only to find I'd been fleeced because it was illegal and I was lucky to sell it later for $400. In short, I keep believing in people and it's nice to come across honest people for a change.

Best Regards,
K. B.

FINAL EDITORIAL COMMENT

K. B. has developed into a successful advanced black-jack player and I owe him a debt of gratitude for

motivating me to develop the BLACKJACK CORRE-
SPONDENCE COURSE. As this book is published, K. B.
continues to play blackjack in the Caribbean, South
America and, once or twice a year, in Las Vegas. We still
correspond but have yet to meet in person.

Those readers planning a trip to the Caribbean should
use the betting schedule from Chapters 6 and 13—one
similar to the Las Vegas Shoe Game.

CHAPTER 18
Blackjack Trip to the Bahamas— Freeport*

Early last year I was doing my usual losing bit at Resort's baccarat table when a "big shooter" sat down next to me and asked how the shoe was running. I showed him my "scorecard," and he noticed the two different-color pens I use.

"You must have read Lyle Stuart's book," he remarked. I replied that I had indeed read it *(Casino Gambling for the Winner)* and thought it to be the best of its type. We chatted a bit, introduced ourselves and the talk eventually turned to blackjack.

---

*This chapter is by Bill Channels—one of Jerry Patterson's BLACKJACK CLINIC graduates. The material is reprinted from Stanford Wong's *Blackjack Newsletter* (March 1980: Vol. 2, No. 3. Box 1144, La Jolla, CA 92038).

"Have you read Revere?" he asked.

"Pete (that's what I'll call him), I've read all the books on BJ, but you can see I'm still playing baccarat."

"But you know," Pete said, "BJ is the only game you can beat if you're good enough."

Of course I knew that, hell, everyone knows that, but the key is, *if you're good enough.* There was my problem.

Pete continued. "Jerry Patterson runs a blackjack school and I've heard it's good. You ought to check it out."

I did, and what Pete said was true—Patterson's course was solid, so I signed up. I completed the course and set a goal for myself—become good enough at BJ to travel the world and play with my winnings paying the way. I didn't want to do it full time; no BJ game is going to pay me like the multi-national corporation where I work as a Marketing VP, but I wanted to at least play as well as a pro.

After a couple of hundred hours of play in A.C., I had the numbers, knew most of the tricks, and started winning—big. I knew then that I was going to vacation only in places with casinos and I was going to go on a lot of vacations.

Playing BJ for big stakes is fun when you're a card counter. You have to look like you're having fun, win or lose, because the pit bosses and floormen are suspicious of anyone varying his bets, let alone someone who varies his bets and wins! The answer to their paranoia is camouflage. Not painting your face various shades of green— not that type of camouflage (though I would do it if it worked!). No, what I'm talking about is playing winning BJ, counting cards, *beating them at their own game*—and all the while having them think you're just another loser.

That kind of camouflage is tough to put out—but you have to do it. Those who are good have the key to the Treasure Room; those who aren't good don't need a cover; they'll lose and that's the best cover of all—expensive, though. Getting back to playing blackjack around the world, if you like beaches and palm trees, Freeport in the Bahamas has them. Me, I like blackjack, and they have just that—at El Casino, a Moorish-style edifice next to the Princess Towers Hotel.

But it sure isn't A.C.! The game is considerably different—four decks, double only on 9, 10 and 11 and no double after splitting pairs. When my first hand was a 15 against the dealer's 10, I instinctively said "surrender." The young English dealer's reply was, "You American chaps won that war two hundred years ago, and now here you are trying to turn yourself in." At that point I remembered the surrender rule isn't used in the Bahamas. The other primary variation to A.C. is that the dealer, when his up-card is a 10 or ace, checks or "peeks" to see if he has blackjack. Of course, if he has an ace-up, you can take insurance.

This "peeking" speeds the game up considerably, and the more hands you play, the more you win. So there I was, in the magical Bahamas—snow left behind, turquoise ocean, sugar-white beaches, and a casino where I didn't care if they barred me for counting cards. Time to make some money.

Card counting seems to be of little concern to the supervisory personnel at El Casino; a party atmosphere prevails and everyone was having fun. So was I; jumping my bets from one hand of $5 to two of $50 when the count went up was great fun! And believe me, I wasn't hurting them—the tourists who visit the Bahamas are terrible BJ players, and with a house percentage of 0.6% against the basic strategy player, the only way you can win in the Bahamas is to be *very* lucky or count cards. Almost every hand someone would split 10s, stand on ace-5 or hit a 14 against a 6. Though some of these moves could be proper at times, these weren't counters, so they lost like crazy. Why should some pit boss get upset if I won a couple of thousand? They didn't!

Anyway, the place was packed, the $5 tables were full and the quarter tables were nearly full. Those were the perfect conditions for "backcounting." No, it's not checking out the tanned backs of all the lovely ladies down there, though any time spent in that endeavor isn't wasted—backcounting is standing behind a table counting the cards until the deck is favorable, then sitting down until the shoe runs out or the deck goes minus. In A.C. that's a quick way to get barred—in the Bahamas either no one noticed or if they did, they didn't care. Such nice chaps! I really felt free in the Bahamas playing aggressively with little or no camouflage. At the worst they would bar me, and who cared? El Casino may see me once a year, in A.C. they see me once a week, minimum. There's a lot more to lose by being barred in A.C.

For the three days I was there, I had an ideal game; no "heat," almost half a deck cut off in the shoe and plenty of wide bet-variation possible. Everyone was friendly—the dealers were effusive with their thanks when I tipped them, the pit boss gave me some souvenir decks of cards and everyone expressed his sympathy at my "losses." What more could I ask?

If you are an experienced card counter, I heartily recommend a trip to the Bahamas. For those of you who want to go, below is some additional information.

But do me one favor—be gentle; don't get greedy. It's a good game, do your part to keep it that way.

El Casino: Freeport, Bahamas. Blackjack tables 28; casino edge 0.6%; decks 4; good comments 17; bad comments db 9. *(Key:* db double-down only on 9,10,11; 17: dealer stands on soft 17.

Jackets are not required.

Taxis are expensive; the Princess Towers adjoins El Casino and the Bahamas Princess is across the street—I would stay at one of them.

The casino opens at 9 A.M. for slot play and at 12 noon for the table games.

Chapter 19
Blackjack Trip to the Bahamas— Nassau *

After a successful trip to Freeport, Bahamas, last year, I've had a warm spot in my heart for BJ in the Bahamas, so I thought I'd check out Nassau. Freeport offers a fairly good game of BJ and that's about it. Nassau, on the other hand, was like visiting another world. It has a great nightlife, terrific tourist attractions and two casinos. The blackjack there is great—better than Freeport—and profitable, as you'll see.

I have to admit that it's a real gas to travel all over with blackjack paying the way. Atlantic City is my "homebase,"

*This chapter is by Bill Channels—one of Jerry Patterson's BLACKJACK CLINIC graduates.

but I like going to other places to play. Nassau has rapidly become one of my favorite stopping places: three or four days in Nassau simply isn't enough. On this trip I took the wife along so all my time wasn't spent playing BJ. However, I did average six hours per day at the tables. Nassau is fun, romantic and "veddy Continental"; the locals were very cordial and service, though slow by American standards, was at least bearable.

On our first night in Nassau, we stopped in at the Playboy Casino, which is in the Ambassador Hotel at Cable Beach, about four miles outside Nassau. The Playboy Casino is quite small, only twenty BJ tables, of which no more than fourteen were in operation while I was there. As advertised, they have "Bunny" dealers who come mostly from England and seem to be rather inexperienced. Because of its small size, there are no pit bosses per se. Off-duty dealers act as floor supervisors, so very little attention is paid to what you do—as long as the game is honest, they don't seem to care what happens! For a card counter, these are great conditions; you can vary your bets at will, a key to overcoming the house advantage. The BJ rules at the Playboy are: four decks (one and one half decks cut off), double only on 9, 10 and 11, resplit pairs (except aces), and double on 9, 10 and 11 after splitting. There is no surrender and if the dealer has a 10 or ace-up, she checks her hole-card to see if she has a "blackjack." Of course, if she has an ace-up, insurance is available. One oddity is that when the cut card comes out, play is stopped, the remaining cards are reshuffled, then the hand is completed. This dealing technique can change the count of the deck quite radically, so you have to stay aware of the positioning of the cut card to avoid being caught with a large bet out only to see a great count shuffled away. Once the cut card comes out, you cannot change your bet, and you must play the next hand. With all this in mind, I found a seat at a $25 table (maximum bet is $500) and handed four $100 bills to Bunny Farah. She gave me sixteen greens ($25 chips) and used a small mechanical counter affixed to the table to record the "drop." This little idea was interesting because in most casinos that figure is written down by the floorperson, which can give them an idea of how you're doing— something a card counter *doesn't* want! I started playing and losing right from the start. Within a half-hour I was down $800 and was trying to smile. Good ol' Bunny Farah was making impossible hands look easy and I was getting trash; they weren't hands—they were feet. Anyway, I reminded myself that I had the advantage and vowed to "hang tough." Just as I was pushing out another $500 in cash, the wife came excitedly up to my table.

"I have to talk to you," she said. Naturally, I thought she needed more money, so I reached for my wallet.

"No, it's not that! I just have to speak with you, that's all." I got up and we walked over to a quiet corner.

"I found my first tell," she exclaimed.

A tell! It's a fact you can win at BJ by counting cards— we all know that. But what most people don't know is you can sometimes win without counting—and dealer tells are one of the primary tools. A tell occurs when a dealer checks his hole-card (when he has a 10- or ace-up) to see if he has a blackjack and through some nonverbal way gives you an idea what the hole-card is. It may be a facial expression or something like that, and it may not always be accurate, but it could be a real help. The tell my wife found was worth investigating; and was it a beauty!

She took me over to a table where a young man was dealing (bunny shortage, I guess) and told me to watch what happened when he had an ace-up. A few hands later he got an ace and rather than asking for insurance, he peeked at his hole-card, started to turn it over to show his "natural" and *then* remembered to ask for insurance. Now, there was an easy decision to make! According to Stanford Wong's *Winning Without Counting* ($50 from Pi Yee Press, Box 1144, La Jolla, CA 92038), knowing when to insure with this type of accuracy is worth 2.4%. With a house edge of .5%, this tell would give me a 1.9% edge without counting! Add counting to that and my edge would be about 3%. Time to make some money. This dealer was at a $5 table (max. bet $300), so it took me a while to get a seat, but his tell was as regular as clockwork, for the time being. I knew it wouldn't last forever, though. Sooner or later he was going to remember to ask for insurance *before* peeking, and poof!—a good tell would be gone. It did last long enough for me to get a seat, dig out and show a profit, but for the rest of my stay I never saw that dealer again. Too bad; he was neat!

Tells like this are impossible to use in A.C. because the dealer doesn't check the hole-card, but in the Caribbean and in Vegas, the "peek" is used and an alert player may find a playable tell. In fact, many professional BJ players will try to cultivate such a tell with the idea of making it a permanent part of a dealer's actions. This may not seem to be "cricket" to some of you (especially if you're a pit

boss), but all you're doing is acting on information the
dealer is providing at no cost to everyone at the table.
Now if you bribe a dealer to give a tell, you're cheating,
and I'm against that. However, if a dealer accidentally
exposes his hole-card, do you think I'm going to ignore it?
No way! Nor am I going to ignore a tell. I may or may not
try to cultivate it, but I can guarantee that if a dealer has a
tell, I'm going to fight for a seat at his or her table. A
recent story was published in Wong's *Blackjack Newsletter*
about a professional BJ player who found an interesting
tell. This dealer was so intent on winning every hand that
when she had a good hole-card she "glowed like an
angel." If she had a 2 to 7 under, she appeared uncom-
fortable and dissatisfied. The pro that discovered the tell
passed the information on to "Peter," another pro. Peter
quickly went to the table only to find that the tell was
gone! Now the dealer had only a bored, faraway look that
never changed. Peter figured this dealer (by now nick-
named "Angel") only "told" her hole-card when she
wanted to beat a specific player—probably a player she
didn't like. He figured the best thing to do was to get
Angel to hate him. On the next hand Peter bet $50 for
himself and 50¢ for Angel. He won the hand, Angel paid
his bet off and paid off her 50¢ bet. Peter then picked up
the tip along with his own winnings, put the tip in his
pocket and stuck his tongue out at Angel! That was it—
she wanted to destroy him financially as well as physically.
And guess what happened to her tell? Right! It magically
reappeared because Angel now had someone she really
wanted to beat. Peter continues to act "like Superass" [his

own words] whenever he plays at Angel's table to rein-force her tell. Ingenious BJ, you must admit!

However, back to the Bahamas. On my second day there I went by myself to the Paradise Island Casino, which is run by our Resorts International friends. It's a nice place, very Vegas-looking and much larger than the Playboy Casino, with thirty-two BJ tables. The rules are the same as at Playboy, except you cannot resplit pairs, the max. bet at all tables is $300 and you can double on a *soft* 9, 10 or 11, i.e., A,10. While your play is more closely watched than at Playboy, nonetheless wide bet-variation is tolerated. At Paradise Island they do not stop dealing when the cut card comes out; the round continues until finished, then they shuffle as in A.C. The casino opens at noon with two $2 tables, the rest are $5 minimums. Later in the evening four $25 tables opened in the baccarat pit. I played there for a few hours, had a good session and hit the beach.

Later that evening my wife and I went back to the Playboy Casino to see what the action was. By now I was used to their game and was winning fairly steadily with little attention and no heat from the floor personnel. Part of my winning was because BJ in the Bahamas is played much faster—by "peeking," the dealers expose their blackjacks right away rather than after everyone plays his hand, as in A.C. That, combined with pressure from the management on the dealers to deal quickly, gave me at least twice the number of hands per hour that I get in A.C. With card counting, the more you play, the more you win. Nice, huh?

CHAPTER 20
Blackjack Trip to Puerto Rico

The weather is getting colder outside and warmer inside the Atlantic City casinos. I was considering a number of destinations for my next blackjack trip when an ad in the local newspaper caught my eye: "Casino Latino Player Package. A sure bet for up to five luxurious nights at the Condado Holiday Inn and Casino at San Juan, Puerto Rico. You and your companion have a standing invitation to spend six days—five nights at San Juan's beautiful seaside hotel and casino. (If you qualify.)"

This junket sounds like a perfect trip to me except for one small detail—the blackjack game in San Juan is one of the world's worst. The casino has an advantage of nearly 1% over the basic strategy player. A betting spread of 8 or 12 to 1 would yield a player advantage of less than 1%. However, I had heard that the casinos rarely change

192

decks and so it might just be possible to read warped cards and gain a higher advantage with this kind of strategy. (Reading warped cards in a blackjack game and using this information to gain an advantage is explained in Stanford Wong's *Winning Without Counting:* Pi Yee Press, Box 1144, La Jolla, CA 92038, $50). As I needed a vacation anyway, I decided to take a shot on this junket for a fairly small bankroll of $5000. Even with the bad rules and assuming that I could not read the warps, I knew that the casino would have a very small chance of beating me.

So, Nancy, Bryn (my son) and I packed our bags and jumped aboard a nonstop, wide-bodied jet bound for Puerto Rico on the day before Thanksgiving. We stepped off the plane into 86 degree weather, but I would see very little sun on this trip.

After checking into the hotel I didn't even bother to unpack my bags before rushing down to the casino. The junket requires me to play with a $5000 bankroll and make minimum $50 bets for two and a half hours per day. You can play against a $5000 line of credit or deposit $5000 in cash with the cashier. I choose the latter course of action. In order to buy chips I write markers (which are the same as checks) against my $5000. One disadvantage of this junket is that I am restricted from taking this $5000 to any other casino. When I win money I do not cash in my chips for cash—I cash in my chips for credit slips which will be paid off on my last day of the junket.

The Condado Holiday Inn Casino is very small by Atlantic City standards. It has fourteen blackjack tables. The rules are doubling down only on 11, splitting any pair, no resplitting, no surrender, dealer stands on soft

17, more than one card may be taken to a split ace. When pairs are split, both of the new hands are dealt a card before the player plays out the hand. The dealer cuts off about one-fourth to three-quarters of a deck from the four-deck game. When the cut card is dealt, the game is stopped until after the dealer shuffles. Two discard trays are used. There is no discernible pattern evident about how the dealer places the discards in either of the discard trays. The dealers deal very fast and in many cases attempt to play your hand for you if the decision is obvious. This can be somewhat disconcerting if you have a soft 18 against an up-card of 10 and the dealer passes you by.

The casino is very casual about money. There is no cashier. Money is exchanged for chips at the table and vice versa. When the dealer cashes a bill in exchange for chips, he doesn't have to announce this fact to the floorperson.

My first session ended exactly even.

There are two problems with this game which I have not yet solved: (1) some of the dealers pick up a breaking hand before I can see the break card, (2) some of the dealers ask for insurance before they deal the hole-card and do not give me a chance to read the warp in the hole-card. This latter problem can be solved by asking for time, but this doesn't always work because the dealer will give me the time, but his hand will be poised ready to peek, hiding the hole-card as I'm making the decision. In the second session I had a serious downswing and had cashed $2000 before receiving some good cards and recouping to finish down a total of $400. I am betting a maximum of $200, which yields a ruin factor of about 1% for the $5000 bank. ("Ruin factor" is the probability, usually expressed as a percent, of losing your entire bankroll.) I don't push the $200 out unless I have a win on a $100 bet and the true count is 6 or higher. I have been getting some fantastically high true-counts with a half-deck-cut card.

Later, after watching a flamenco show in the hotel cabaret, I decided to have one more go. The highlight of the session was a $200 blackjack. Nancy was given her $100 worth of free chips and then we spent an enjoyable twenty minutes hearing cockfighting stories from a friendly floorperson. I ended this first day stuck about $800.

My play does not go well on Thursday evening. I suffer an immediate downswing of about $1000, recoup to $300 ahead, and then the situation once again reverses itself and I end up the day down about $930.

My overall status is now down $1100 in markers plus the $680 in returned airfare and $100 out-of-pocket at the Carib Hilton Casino. I am not discouraged. I remember Stanford Wong's comment as he discusses it in *Blackjack in Asia* after losing over $10,000 in a twenty-four-hour period: "Ice water is coursing through my veins."

The Friday-evening session begins later after an extended delay at the airport waiting for Nancy and Bryn to return from a shopping spree in the Virgin Islands—St. Thomas. The highlight of this session is splitting a pair of 10s against a 5 (with a true of 5) and winning on both hands with the dealer breaking. The blackjack dealers here are extremely fast. They always play your hand for you if your total is 10 or less. It is interesting to watch a dealer deal to a split hand. The cards are moved apart, he

deals two cards, one to each hand, and then comes back
and hits the first hand until the total is 11 or more. If the
total is 11 he places a card face down against the 11,
waiting for your double-down decision. If the total is 10
or less he keeps hitting until the total is 12 or more and
then stands, waiting for you to make a decision. The
whole thing happens within split seconds and leaves the
player in a somewhat bewildered state.

The cards run very well for me this evening. Five times
out of six when doubling an 11 versus 10 and watching
the dealer turn over the 20, I pull the 10 for a perfect 21.
My overall status at the end of Friday is in the black—
about $300 ahead.

On Saturday, Nancy and Bryn go snorkling, which
leaves me free to visit some of the other San Juan casinos.

La Concha is a very small casino, having only five or six
blackjack tables. You are not allowed to play two hands,
although you are allowed to play a full table. All of the
tables except one have a regular four-deck discard tray.
Most of the dealers cut the deck right around the half-
deck mark. As in the Holiday Inn, the dealers at La
Concha have the annoying habit of scooping up the
player's breaking card with the rest of the hand before
those players sitting near third base can see the card.

I get into my first argument at the El San Juan. The
dealer passes me by on a soft 18 vs. 9 and deals to the
third base player before I can signal my intention to hit. I
call over the pit boss and complain bitterly. He won't even
listen to my complaint and backs up the dealer totally. In
the meantime the cards are scooped up. The game goes
on. No one pays attention to my continuing complaints.
Totally different from Atlantic City, where the player gets

a fair hearing and the benefit of the doubt.

The Saturday-evening session is highly successful. It brings my total trip winnings to $1925. I am doing considerable table-hopping trying to find the tables with a high positive count. Many of the dealers are dealing down to the quarter-deck mark and some even below that. The general policy on the cut cards seems to be about a half to three-quarters of a deck from the end during the afternoon and about a quarter to a half with a bias toward the quarter-deck mark in the evening. One can readily find dealers dealing to the quarter-deck mark during the evening shift.

I am betting from $50 to $400 ($200 on each of two hands) during this last session with no heat whatsoever. I am dealt some interesting hands. I split a pair of 10s (with a "true" of 12) with a $200 bet out and am dealt a 9 to one and a 10 to the other. The dealer breaks. On one shoe I get greedy and am caught with two $200 bets on the table when the cut card came out. I am dealt a 2 to 1 hand and a 9 to the other. Needless to say, while the dealer is shuffling, I feel naked with all that money on the table and nothing I can do to reduce the size of my bet with the shoe restored to the negative 1% level. After shuffling, the dealer completes the round, dealing himself a 5-up and myself a 12 to the first hand and a pair of 9s to the second hand. Naturally I split the 9s and put another $200 on the table. I now have a total of $600 on the table with the dealer showing a 5. I draw a 7 to the first 9 and a 6 to the second 9 so now I am sitting with a total of three stiff hands. The only way I can win is if the dealer breaks. The dealer turns over a 3 for a total of 8. He hits the 8 with a 3 and now is sitting with a total of 11. My mind already sees the face card being dealt to give the dealer a total of 21 and wipe out my $600 when, lo and behold, he deals himself a 3 for a total of 14 and then hits his hand with the most beautiful face card I have ever seen. I let out an excited yell and bang my fist on the table to express my sheer exhilaration. A twelve-hundred-dollar swing! This is a hand I should not have won but did and the hand more than makes up for a number of hands I should have won but didn't.

I am playing with some tremendously high true-counts in this final session. It seems logical that a quarter-deck-cut card is worth even more than is yielded by Arnold Snyder's Blackjack Formula. Any time that you are able to divide your running count by less than 1 to effectuate a multiplication, and as that multiplier increases up to 4, you are getting a tremendous advantage. The game is certainly more fun to play when these kinds of high true-counts occur. And they certainly occur with much more frequency than in the Atlantic City six-deck game, where the smallest divisor is 2. My final calculations for the Puerto Rican game are as follows (using Arnold Snyder's *Blackjack Formula*: R. G. Enterprises, 2000 Center St. #1067, Berkeley, CA 94204, $100):

		Player Advantage (%) One-Half- Deck Cut	Player Advantage (%) One-Fourth- Deck Cut
SPREAD	4 to 1	0.164	0.3
	8 to 1	0.6	0.758
	12 to 1	0.936	1.09

If you go to Puerto Rico on this junket, play an 8 to 1 spread (bet $50 to $200—two hands) in the evening when you can get a quarter-deck cut. You will enjoy a small advantage. I believe that a 12 to 1 spread would be too obvious and would mark you as a counter.

Nancy and I leave the casino on very good terms with the floor people. Mr. Vargas, the assistant manager and a very tough-looking but suave-acting dude, was very courteous and kind to us when we cashed out the chips at the end of our play on Saturday evening.

We also say goodbye to our other friends on the floor. Really a nice feeling to be on such good terms with casino personnel.

SECTION VI
Women in Blackjack

Chapter 21
The Advantages
of the Woman Blackjack Player,
by Nancy Patterson

About fifteen years ago I discovered the very best profession for a woman—and I was really ahead of the times. That field was sales—not clothing-store type of sales, but competing with men in the intangible-sales field. I knew I had a specialized talent for sales because I liked people and I was careful to get into an area where male chauvinism in potential customers would not hurt me. I did well and enjoyed my work tremendously. Now women in creative sales are accepted in most companies, but I'm again in a new field for women.

Playing blackjack is a very unusual profession for a

woman—in fact even for a man. But it is a wonderful
opportunity to turn the tables on some of the world's male
chauvinists and actually use their attitudes to make more
money than one could without them.

The rest of this chapter is off limits to those pit bosses
and casino floor people who would fit into the category of
being even a mild male chauvinist. Please go back to your
tables and continue to believe that "Women are too dumb
to count" or that "Women play on hunches and raise their
bets on feelings."

The male chauvinism philosophy is best expressed by
a person most directly involved—a female dealer who
worked in a Las Vegas casino for four years. I asked Lyn
what the floor and pit people thought about women
blackjack players and if they looked for female card
counters. Her reply was emphatically negative. She said if
a woman is playing for high stakes, they believe that she
has a wealthy husband or lover who likes to throw his
money around. Dealers, in fact, have been known to help
female players by passing them by when the dealer knows
he has a small card underneath and a good chance of
breaking.

Lyn said, "A woman can get away with a betting spread
of from $5 to $100—without attention of the casino
personnel!" They enjoy having women play at their tables
and will probably be very friendly, sometimes even flir-
tatious. It is really fun for me to sit at a blackjack table and
know exactly how to play the hands and when to put out
larger bets while the pit boss is thinking of me as just
another dumb broad. In the meantime, one is legally
taking money out of the casino right from under their
noses.

For you guys who are reading this chapter, we women are really sorry that with the same bankroll to work with, we can make more money per hour than you can. But that's the breaks. I can suggest one thing to help you—train your girlfriend or your wife to count cards. Besides, all good card counters make really good money regardless of whether they're a man or a woman. Let me explain why a woman has a higher advantage than a man. Remember that in card counting you bet your minimum bet when the count is negative, up to your maximum when the count is very high. Ideally, you could sit at a $5 table and bet $5 when the count is low and work up to $200 or $300 when it is high.

But that is a very impractical betting spread and one of the best ways for a man to get barred. Now, as it happens, the pit bosses do not worry about women card counters because there are so few right now, and a woman can usually get away with a fantastic betting spread. The quicker you can get the big bets on the table when the count goes high, the more money you make. Men need to be more careful so that the pit bosses do not suspect them of counting.

There are many desirable aspects of being a female card counter, and some of the graduates of the BLACK-JACK CLINIC have shared not only their results but some of the more interesting stories of being a woman in a very unusual profession. There is a strong feeling among them that many more women should learn to count and enjoy playing blackjack as a full- or part-time career. What else could you do that is as exciting, glamorous, financially rewarding and flexible enough to fit into any schedule? Remember also, you are your own boss.

I have talked to hundreds of women on the phone who have called our New Jersey office with questions about the course. The two main questions are, "Can we make money?" and "Do you really think I can learn to count? After all, there are six decks." I was really put to the task by one very capable-sounding woman—for privacy reasons let's call her Michelle. My conversation with Michelle really stripped me of all my normal sales ability. To answer this person, I could not just look at generalities. In fact, she helped me realize that, yes, I really did believe that many other women besides me could go to the casinos and steadily take home a good profit. I knew there was no problem in learning to count six decks with the proper instruction. But when she asked her question, my breath stopped momentarily and I couldn't answer until I had really given it some thought.

Michelle said, "I earn $45,000 a year and I am thinking of taking your course and quitting my job to play blackjack instead. Can I earn the same $45,000 a year at the casinos?"

I still remember the overwhelming sense of responsibility I felt. Most of the people I talk to about our course are not thinking of giving up their jobs (remember, they are 95% married men with families or singles wanting something like a new sports car), they want to use card counting at blackjack to make extra money and/or are just plain tired of losing. When you are talking to a man who is losing a hundred, two hundred a month or more at the casino, it is very easy for him to get excited about the prospect of being armed with card-counting and money-management skills so that he can start a lifetime of taking home his profits. Most of our students do extremely well. We know because we poll our graduates every three months to see how they are doing. Anyway, back to Michelle. If I said yes, a woman who had never been to a casino at all, who read Jerry's book and became interested, would quit her $45,000-a-year job and plan to make that $45,000 at the blackjack tables.

There is one thing I can tell you for sure. If she had been a he, I would undoubtedly have told him *not* to quit his job. The reason is that at the time of this writing, the casinos are still able to bar card counters from playing blackjack. *It is not illegal for you to play,* but they have the right to ask you to play only the games they know can't be beaten. And, if a man were to play every day, the chances are much higher that he would be barred. We teach people in our course how not to look like a card counter, and how to look like a progressive bettor and loser, but I can't predict how well they practice what we teach. Because Michelle is a woman, her chances of being barred are probably less than half of a man's—and we have had very few of our players barred. I asked Michelle what kind of a bankroll she had to start with, because the amount of money you win depends on the amount you put on the table. (Your profit is 1.5% of all the money you put on the table in the long run.) She said bankroll was no problem, and I gulped a large breath and gave her the go-ahead.

The outcome: Michelle was a very good student. She practiced. Good students are measured by the speed with which they count down six decks and use variations on the basic strategy. After graduating, she wanted to put $2000 or $3000 into her bankroll, but her teacher (our marvelous head instructor, Bob) told her not to. He said for her to start with an $800 bankroll and to gain confidence in her abilities. In all fairness, I must give you a comment Michelle wrote to me when I asked her about "Women's Place in Professional Blackjack." She said she loves it, but she was doubtful about other women and said, "Most have no true concept of having made large sums of money, let alone having won it," and "Few women presently oriented to higher-than-average finances are willing to make a career change to long- versus short-term gains." I must add to that. She finished the course in April 1981, and her starting bankroll of $800 grew to $10,670 in just a few months. That is part of the reason that she is quite happy. In fact, I have been very careful to change her name and to put nothing in this book that would endanger her playing career. She and her husband play together on weekends or evenings, and they are enjoying it tremendously. Today, I would no longer hesitate to recommend that a woman play professional blackjack no matter what amount of money she would need to make. As her bankroll goes up, so does her hourly win rate. We have many graduates making $50 an hour and better. (Obviously, then, you don't play every day—you don't need to.)

Aside from being able to get the bets out without any heat, here are two more examples of advantages you have as a woman that a man would never get away with. One of our students, Diane, told me not long ago that this past summer she frequented one particular casino almost daily for a month—a definite way to get barred under normal conditions. Not only did the pit bosses welcome her (being much prettier to look at and more pleasant to talk to than a guy), but she also received two or three meal comps every week, some of them for the gourmet restaurant. What makes her story even more incredible was that she was a small bettor, betting only $5 to $20. The second advantage pertains to the Nevada casinos. Just smile at the dealers and it is possible they will give you a hint as to whether you should hit or stay. Unlike Atlantic City, the dealers peek at their face-down card. If, for instance, you have a 16 and the dealer up-card is a 10, you could bust if you take a hit. The nice dealer might say something to you like, "You look pretty good to me, honey." What he's saying is that he doesn't have a 7 or better under that 10 and will have to take a hit and may go bust himself, so you should stay. I'd say that's right nice of him.

The instructors advise every student to start out with a small ($600 to $800) bankroll, even if they can afford to begin with more. While you are getting comfortable with the casino atmosphere and gaining confidence in your play, your small bankroll is gaining in size. If you can afford then to add to it and begin placing larger bets, fine. If not, you simply allow your bankroll to grow at its normal optimal rate. Your per-hour win rate grows in proportion to your bankroll, and your bankroll grows in proportion to your per-hour win rate. It's a never-ending circle of making more money.

The hourly win rate of an $800 bankroll is the same if you play as little as twice a month or as frequently as twice a week, so the rate at which your bankroll grows depends upon the time you can spend at the casinos. If you are a mother with school-age children, you could possibly change your schedule around to be free up to two days a week or more. If you are a full-time working woman, with a heavy schedule one week and a light schedule the next, where else could you find such a flexible part-time venture?

To all of you men who are reading this chapter, I want you to know that I am really not as much of a women's libber as I sound. I know there are innumerable men who fully believe in the capabilities of women; in fact, I am married to one. I also know that not all male pit bosses think the way I chided them about. I probably sound like I do in this chapter because it really bothers me to sit at a blackjack table and watch so many women throw their money away because they play badly. I can't tell you how many times I have sat there, winning, and watched as women came to the table to get more money from their husbands for their slot-machine mania. I really feel it is because they think: "It is impossible for me to learn how to count six decks," and "You need a *fantastic* memory to remember all those cards." These quotes are from women who believed these erroneous assumptions until they found out the truth. They learned that they don't need to be even good in mathematics—as long as they can add and subtract 1 from a number, they can count. And six decks are as easy to count as one—you just keep doing it longer. The truth is, the women who learned are a part of a small minority who became interested and asked questions. They now enjoy a new status. Many take their husbands on casino-paid vacations—junkets—or just pay for the trips out of their winnings.

I'd like to give you another career woman's point of

view on playing blackjack. In fact, I asked Christina L to write up her experiences for you so you could get it straight from the player instead of from my writing about her. She can count so well that she glances around the casino, engages floor people in conversations, and then quickly scans the table for the count.

Chapter 22
Case Study of a Female Card Counter, by Christina L

My career, so to speak, in blackjack started last winter when my boyfriend came to the apartment one night with two books: Jerry's *Blackjack's Winning Formula* and Ken Uston's *Two Books on Blackjack,* and more or less announced, "You should take it up. You'd be good at it!" He had been following Jerry's columns for some time, has two friends who are counters, and *he* was convinced it worked. His reasons for assuming I would do so well were my mathematical ability and my ability to concentrate for long periods of time. I was not terribly thrilled. Yes, math was always fun and easy for me. However, I've been out of school eighteen years and math is only a small part of my job. Yes, I could concentrate heavily for long periods of time, but only if I liked something. That's where the skepticism of this whole scheme came in to play. I hated card games. The last time I played cards was when I was about nine or ten and rummy was in. After playing one game, boredom would set in and I was off to something more fun or productive. Card games were dumb and, being an active person, sitting still for long periods doing something unproductive or boring was not to my liking. The sum total of my knowledge of a deck of cards and the game of blackjack was this: a normal deck had 52 cards, four suits, and numbers from 2 through 10, J, Q, K and A; blackjack was a game of whoever could come closest to 21 without going over. Period.

Only through sheer courtesy to my boyfriend did I decide to at least read the two books he bought. About eleven the following night I decided to force myself to read one or two chapters before retiring. At four in the morning, after finishing both books, I started reviewing them. That day at lunch I purchased six decks of cards and some chips so I could start practicing that night.

What changed my mind so drastically? Two things. First, playing this card game would be productive— MONEY. I'm not sure about you, but I like it and would like to have more. The second was my belief in why it would work. It has been statistically proven over and over again by some of the greatest mathematical minds that with the givens (the dealer must hit to 17, there are only 52 cards in a deck, and there are only 4 aces in a deck, etc.), if you make certain decisions based on your cards and the dealer's up-card, and you bet more or less money when more high or low cards have been dealt, then you will have an advantage, i.e., you will relieve the casinos of some of their money. I never delved into the mathematics concerning the game, but I do believe in them. I also believe in mathematical sciences though I may not understand them.

For example, Archimedes' principle is a mathematical formula that will determine whether or not a particular item will float or sink in a particular liquid. Would you have to know this formula in order to place a bet on a beach ball versus a metal ball as to which would float? Certainly not! Do you believe that you will not float off this planet into space? That an object gains speed the farther it has to fall? That if you put a full or partially full can of spray paint in a fire, after a certain amount of time it will explode? You certainly do. Do you understand or have any knowledge of the mathematics behind it? Probably not. Do you have to? No. You do not need to know anything about statistics—but you must have the confidence to believe it. I did.

With the belief and visions of dollar signs dancing in my head, I signed up for Jerry's blackjack course. By the day the course was to start, I was glad I wore my Ban. I was still highly excited about the end results ($), believed in my statistics, and believed that if Pavlov's dog could be trained, so could I. My nervousness emerged from two areas. The worst being that between the time I signed up for the course and the day it was to start I had bought out the bookstores on every book of blackjack they carried. I tried to learn and understand everything there was to know in a very short period of time and without any practice or actual experience with the basics. For the most part, it was *Playing Blackjack as a Business,* Revere's book, that intimidated me. Filled with dozens of color-coded tables, I was starting to wonder how long it would take to memorize all of it and if the effort and time spent would be worth it dollar-wise. The other part of my nervousness was the time factor. I am involved in a number of outside interests and ventures. A number of those commitments or interests could be curtailed for the duration of the course, others could not. I assumed I would need to put in five times the study time as anyone else because I had never played blackjack in a casino. I wasn't comfortable with cards yet, and I could not shuffle a deck without dropping at least some of them. The high probability that I would be the only woman in the class did not bother me. I am, and almost always have been, involved in many areas of business, sports and interests that are about 90% male type areas. Being born the classic tomboy (I still am), I was never uncomfortable around men. My discomfort was caused by assuming that, since they were men, they knew card games, were obviously good at blackjack, had played a lot and were adroit at card handling. I would be equally if not more uncomfortable in a cooking class of all women, knowing that they could boil an egg or bake a potato without looking in a cookbook. They would assume I could also. I can't.

A minor area of concern was that I would have to put up with cigar smoke—don't all card counters smoke cigars? I figured that I had learned at least enough to fudge my way through that night and would take it from there to play the "catch-up" game. I laughed at myself all the way home that night and couldn't wait to get there so I could go over all drills at least one more time before retiring.

The instructor was excellent and the drills not difficult and yet comprehensive enough that you got that "Yes, I can" feeling. First, they assume that you know nothing about the game. In fact, the less you know, the easier you are to teach, since they would not have to undo any bad habits you've picked up. There were ten people in my class; three of us were women. I understand that in most classes I would have been the only woman, although that is rapidly changing. While there may have been a couple of guys who thought it comical we were there, or that we were throwing our money away, I did not detect it. Possibly because I was too nervous to detect anything.

Of the ten of us, only one of the guys had been playing basic strategy for years and one of the women and two or three of the guys had played blackjack at the casinos. The rest of us were dumbheads. That first night we learned the basics of the game, basic strategy, and some of the whys behind basic strategy. We were given a set of flash cards and some paper drills and a deck of cards to practice on our own the following week. After a twenty-minute coffee break it was off to the back of the room, where we all sat down at a real blackjack table. It was complete with six decks of cards, a shoe and chips (we did not use the chips until later in the course). For those who have never been at a blackjack table, this gave an air of the real. Personally, I thought it was just plain neat.

The following three weeks brought much the same schedule. As soon as each of us arrived individually at the

Academy, we were asked to see our progress forms (many of the drills had to be timed and the number of errors recorded) and asked to do one of the drills for them. Classroom was new techniques and new drills, coffee break, and the blackjack table practical experience. If, during the night, the instructor noted that someone was having a problem, either he or one of the other instructors would give that person some personal attention or advice that he or she should do this or that drill more often. I cannot say enough to praise the excellent step-by-step instruction format, the quality of the instructors, and the quality and quantity of the practice drills we were given to do. They made it all so easy, even though at times I wondered about a particular drill or two. At the end of the four weeks we had a fifth session which consisted of all our card drills laid out on various tables. We were given a sheet to record our time on and proceeded from station to station doing the various drills and then to the blackjack table for some real playing. It was hard to realize that just five weeks prior I was learning that doubling down meant doubling your bet and getting one more card. You must do your practice drills faithfully. To cite extremes, there were two guys in my course who by the fourth week did not even know basic strategy by heart—they admitted they put in only an hour a week practice—on the other hand I came out way at the top of my class, not so much because I needed it, but because I was "hooked." The instructors advise setting aside about an hour a day for practice.

No more stalling; I had graduated with honors. I should have had great confidence in that. Why, then, was I a nervous wreck the day I scheduled my first trip to the casino? I guess because it was my first trip to the real world of casinos—I don't remember. Ten minutes inside and the excitement of it all made me forget my worries. I picked out a table with a slow dealer (so I would be sure to get the count easily), plunked down my money, and practice became the real world. Though they had prepared me to expect to only break even or lose, I was happy I had a winning night for my first trip—$175. It's up and down each night, sometimes win, sometimes lose, sometimes break even. But—you win more than you lose. I've lost $200 in a night, but I've won $260.

The biggest and worse apprehension you will have is that of being spotted as a counter. Everyone gets it. It lasts between fifty and eighty hours. Your impression is that there is a neon sign above your head flashing COUNTER, COUNTER. And that anyone from the pit who so much as glances toward you or walks within five feet of you knows. If you started out as I did with a small ($1000 to $2000) bankroll as they suggest, and are betting $5 to $40 ($2000 bank) with 85% of your bets in the $5 to $15 range, you will realize one night, as I did, how conceited you are thinking they could be that interested in you at those stakes. At that point it will take another five to ten hours to become almost non-paranoid (I don't think you can ever get totally over it) and relaxed. Now, you can start working without fear.

Women can work it far better and to a much greater extent than a man can. First, everyone "knows" only men are counters. They (the casino personnel) may know that there may be a few women counters, but I don't think at this point they consider us a threat. After all—women always play their hunches and cannot be coldly logical, etc., etc., right??? I don't care what the pit bosses think (some of them are women) as long as I come home with the money. You can spread more and more quickly without any or less heat. If a guy jumps $5 to $30 or $40 in one hand the pit people stand by him for some time and watch. If I do the same thing, they come over, look, and walk away—after all, I must be playing a hunch—and that is how I try to look like I'm playing it—a hunch. There are dozens of more instances or games I could mention and I'm still learning and refining. I imagine in another fifty to one hundred hours I'll have these plays down to a tee and refined quite nicely. You still have to be a little cautious, but your chances of getting a lot of heat or being barred are minimal. Also, while I haven't tried my hand at getting meal comps yet, I never had a problem getting my parking tickets comped. This helps defray expenses quite a bit while you're working with a small start-up bankroll.

In summary, this is what you need to take the blackjack course: *Believe that it works; make a commitment to put in the necessary practice time; and, most importantly, form a positive attitude that you can do it and do it well.* I would advise getting a basic grasp of the game by reading this book, but don't get into any of the heavier books unless you have a BA in math—they'll confuse you and it isn't necessary. If anything, I feel most people are skeptical of the math. The math involved is simple. For basic strategy playing you only have to add up to 21—if your hand totals 22 or more they take your cards away. For counting you only have to add 1s or 2s up and down to about 30. If you want to practice adding, buy a deck of cards and deal yourself two cards, add them together, then keep giving yourself more cards until you hit 21 or more. Push those cards aside and start a new hand. For a preliminary practice in counting, start at 1 and count up to 30 and then back down to 1, first by 1s: 1,2,3-30,29,28, etc. Then by 2s: 1,3,5-29,27,25, etc., and 2,4,6-30,28,26, etc. The only big numbers you'll have to add come after the course. They'll be your chips as you take them to the cashier's cage!

SECTION VII

Casino Gaming Services

Section Overview

This section is promotional in nature. Because I am committed to and believe in what I am doing, I have included in Chapter 23 a description of the casino gaming services which I offer. The main service is a BLACKJACK CLINIC in which I instruct beginning to intermediate blackjack players in the application of Blackjack's Winning Formula. I invite reader inquiries on this and other services.

Chapter 24 contains my recommendations and endorsements for casino gaming publications that offer useful information to both occasional and serious gamblers.

Chapter 23
Casino Gaming Services Offered by Jerry L. Patterson

THE BLACKJACK CLINIC

The BLACKJACK CLINIC is a blackjack school which I own and operate. Fifteen hours of instruction are delivered to the student over a five-week period—three hours, one night a week for five weeks.

There are a number of unique and extraordinary features about this school. Here are just a few:

- The students actually win money (I know this because I poll them every three months).

- Anyone can learn to win because I have stripped the mystique from winning blackjack methods (our students come from all walks of life: insurance agents, truck drivers, construction workers, housewives, self-employed businessmen, retired persons, etc.).

• The program is continuous—follow-up service includes a joint visit to a casino, an open line to me and my instructors and periodic review sessions and blackjack updates.

Why, you may be asking, should I take your course on blackjack after just reading your book on blackjack? There are a number of reasons why you should consider it.

• It is difficult to learn from any book, my own included. In a book you can learn *what* winning blackjack is all about, but the key is *how*. How to play basic strategy perfectly without even thinking about it. How to count cards swiftly and accurately. How to bet to maximize your profits and minimize your chances of going broke. How to avoid getting barred.

• The keys to learning how to win are the drills and exercises. In the BLACKJACK CLINIC, there are five basic strategy drills and seven card-counting drills. Doing these drills is easy and fun. You record your progress and gain a keen sense of accomplishment as you watch your skills develop.

• It has been proven that a person learns faster and more effectively in a classroom environment. There are only eight persons per class and each receives all the individual attention he or she needs from me or one of my personally trained instructors. If you need a makeup session, you get it. If you need extra help, you come in early or stay late.

• Beginning to intermediate players will especially benefit from the BLACKJACK CLINIC, although quite a few advanced students have taken it to "fine-tune" their game. No one is held back and each progresses at his own rate of speed.

• Practice is extremely important. We program your home practice sessions for you while you take the CLINIC. In my opinion, it is impossible to learn winning blackjack in a weekend or on four successive nights and then go home and practice correctly with no supervision or feedback.

If you want further information, just check the appropriate box in the Request Form at the end of this section.

THE ADVANCED BLACKJACK CLINIC

Learning how to count cards and using this information to vary your bet size is all you need to know to win at blackjack. You learn this in the BLACKJACK CLINIC. Serious students of the game, who are playing semiprofessionally and desire to put the "icing on the cake," enroll in the ADVANCED CLINIC and learn to gain a small but significant (in terms of dollars won) additional advantage.

The following are the highlights of the ADVANCED CLINIC which I offer to my graduates plus other qualified students:

- You learn that the running count becomes more significant as the shoe is dealt out and the number of decks remaining to be played decreases;

- You learn to use this information to compute a true count used for basic strategy variations and more precise betting decisions;

- You learn to obtain a small but powerful additional advantage by counting aces and using this side count for making more precise insurance, strategy and betting decisions;

- You learn about the power of team play and why the casinos fear well-trained blackjack teams.

If you wish further information, check the appropriate box on the Request Form at the end of this section.

BLACKJACK CORRESPONDENCE COURSE

My first book—*Blackjack: A Winner's Handbook*—sold 12,000 copies in its first two printings. The readers of this book are beginning to intermediate blackjack players from all parts of the country and from foreign countries as well. Many of them have just as much interest in learning to play blackjack the right way as students in this area. Many of the readers wrote to me asking for additional information about my Self-Instruction Course.

Because of this interest I was motivated to duplicate the BLACKJACK CLINIC for use outside my own geographic area. But it had to be done right. I had to personally get involved with each student. Because of its interactive nature, a correspondence course with telephone consultation was the only vehicle that would accomplish this objective.

Thus, the BLACKJACK CORRESPONDENCE COURSE was born. It has proved tremendously successful and has assisted dozens of students to become winning blackjack players. Here are the highlights:

• You can work at your own rate of speed in the privacy of your own home.

• Winning blackjack cannot be learned by reading books; you will gain invaluable practical experience before risking your money in the casinos.

• The entire body of blackjack data is presented to you in an orderly fashion to simplify the learning process.

• You are not working alone. You have access to me at all times via telephone or written correspondence.

• The skills that you will achieve are measurable, and as you record your drill performance, you will see these skills increasing, e.g., you will learn to count down a single deck in less than 30 seconds.

• Once you have achieved your desired level of skills, you

decide upon the winnings you want to achieve. My unique money management methods will show you how to achieve your desired level of winnings.

The one most heard comment from my students is that they are impressed with my honesty, integrity and genuine desire to develop them into an accomplished, money-making blackjack player. This is why I schedule a joint visit to the casino to observe and comment on your play where it really counts—under actual casino conditions.

The BLACKJACK CORRESPONDENCE COURSE is divided into three levels and eight lessons as follows:

Level 1 Skilled Blackjack Player	1. The Basic Strategy 2. The High-Low Point-Count System 3. Basic Money Management 4. Casino Comportment (How not to get barred)
Level II Advanced Blackjack Player	5. Basic Strategy Variations with the True Count 6. Advanced Money Management 7. Side Count of Aces
Level III Team Blackjack Player	8. How to Multiply Your Winnings Through Team Play

Each lesson consists of:

- A detailed lesson plan including background information, complete instructions, assignment descriptions and a statement of the skills to be achieved

- Reading Assignments

- Memory Aids

- Drills—drill sheets, single-deck and multiple-deck drills are used

- An Essay Assignment

- A Quiz

- Questions and Answers

After you complete each lesson you will send all materials to me for my written critique, which will be forwarded to you by return mail. Any out-points will be corrected and you will achieve the projected skill level before you undertake the next lesson. You may stop after achieving your desired level of play—you pay for only those lessons you decide to take.

For further information, check the appropriate box on the Request Form.

MICROCOMPUTER ASSISTED BLACKJACK INSTRUCTION

I have developed a microcomputer, the *Computer Assisted Blackjack Tutor*. This program will sell for less than $100 and can be used with the TRS 80 Model 3 Microcomputer available at the Radio Shack stores for about $900. It is also being programmed to operate on Apple, Commodore and Atari personal computers. It features the High-Low Counting System. The program will allow you to play a game with any number of players, any number of decks, any range of bet sizes and a variable shuffle point. This program is available from Echelon Enterprises, One Britton Place, Voorhees, NJ 08043.

The Computer Assisted Blackjack Tutor features three types of Drill and Practice aids. Each is discussed below.

1. *Basic Strategy Drills.* The player can set indicators to allow him or her to play any kinds of hands:

- The player can ask for random cards to be dealt against random dealer's up-cards.

- The player can fix the dealer's up-card and play random hands.

- The player can ask for pairs or double-down hands to be dealt against fixed ranges of dealer up-cards.

- The player can play soft hands only against fixed or variable dealer up-cards.

The computer remembers those hands giving the player problems and increases the frequency of the problem hands. Any errors are immediately corrected. The player is given a second chance to get the right answer before the computer communicates it to the player.

The player can also play a blackjack game drill and

specify the number of hands to be dealt per round and the number of hands to be played by the player. The computer plays the others.

A full recap is given at the end of the session.

2. *Card-Counting Drill and Practice:* The player can have the cards shown to him or her at variable rates of speed. The objective is to keep the count as fast as the cards flash on the screen.

The player can play a one-to-seven-player game drill and play any or all of the hands—the computer plays the others. The player can specify the speed at which the cards are dealt and whether or not the computer will check for basic strategy.

The player can request to see the correct count at the completion of each hand.

3. *Money Management Drill and Practice:* The player can bet one hand. The computer checks for a correct bet size according to a prescribed money management formula.

Working at his or her own pace, in the privacy of the own home or office, a player with just elementary knowledge of basic strategy, card counting and money management could become a highly skilled blackjack player by using any of the three programs described above. Playing against a computer would enable him or her to gain invaluable experience and achieve any desired level of expertise before risking money at the table.

If you know how to play blackjack but are not satisfied with your progress, consider practicing against a computer. A good program could enable you to reach the level of competency needed to win in the casinos.

BLACKJACK CLINIC FRANCHISES

Because of the success of the BLACKJACK CLINIC in the Philadelphia/South Jersey area, I am expanding it into other areas. The franchise holders I am seeking must be successful blackjack players. What better source than my own students? I have struck such a profitable balance between teaching and playing that I am confident I can duplicate it with other individuals in other areas just as I have with students in this area.

One student is my full-time instructor and teaches the CLINICS in this area. Another teaches weekends in New York—he also holds a full-time job. It's pretty much up to you what you want to do.

Now here is what I can do for you.

1. I will teach you to become a skilled, then advanced, then Team Blackjack Player through the BLACK-JACK CLINIC, ADVANCED CLINIC, or the BLACKJACK CORRESPONDENCE COURSE.
2. I will present you with a BLACKJACK CLINIC Franchise Plan. This plan will show you how, *in your spare time,* you can build a successful BLACKJACK CLINIC in your area. You and I will be partners, and I will be right there with you during the key start-up period to help you implement all of my organizational and instructional materials. Much of the marketing for your area will be done centrally—through my books and newspaper columns.

CASINO GAMES CLINIC

There are of course other casino games besides black-jack. The major difference is that there is no way to overcome the casino advantage in craps, roulette, baccarat, the slot machines or the big six wheel.

Recognizing that there are many players who have an interest in these other games—mainly craps, roulette and baccarat, where the house advantage is the smallest—I have developed the CASINO GAMES CLINIC.

You may enroll for classes in craps, roulette, baccarat or in any combination of the three. Each of these three classes also features a lesson on Blackjack's Basic Strategy.

Here are the highlights:

Craps

• How to play—the "mysteries" are removed. Craps is a remarkably simple game to play.

• How to bet—you will learn the best bets and worst bets and the payoffs and percentages for each.

• How to win—although you can't overcome the casino advantage, we will teach you how to maximize your profits and quit a winner when luck is going your way.

• How to avoid going broke—just as important as winning—you want to avoid the dreadful losing streaks that sometimes beset even the most knowledgeable gamer.

- How to select and play a craps "system"—you will learn which system—or betting methodology—is best for your temperament and bankroll.

- Craps is best learned by applying your newly acquired knowledge in a game situation. You will play on a real craps table with casino-like chips.

Roulette

- How to play—the various types of wagers, their payoffs and house percentages will be explained.

- How to take advantage of the special Atlantic City "in prison" rule which cuts the casino advantage in half.

- How to detect and take advantage of number patterns.

- How to win—we will show you how to select and play a roulette system—systems will help you overcome the house advantage when luck is going your way.

- How to minimize your chances of going broke by utilizing team play.

Baccarat
(taught in both the craps and roulette classes)

- How to play—baccarat is a remarkably simple game to play.

- How to play like the high rollers on a small bankroll—baccarat is an elegant game played in an exclusive, well-appointed, confined area. There is no reason why you should not play with the high rollers even with a limited bankroll.

Blackjack

(taught in both the craps and roulette classes)

- How to play—the fundamentals of the game. How to improve your advantage from −6% to better than even by playing the basic strategy.

- How to make all the blackjack decisions correctly: surrendering, splitting pairs, doubling down, hitting, standing, insuring.

- How to maximize your profits and reduce to virtually zero your chances of going broke.

- As a skilled blackjack player, you will impress your fellow players with your knowledge of the game. With the knowledge you gain, even the third base "hot seat" will be open to you with comfort.

If you are interested in the CASINO GAMES CLINIC, check the appropriate box on the Request Form.

Blackjack: A Winner's Handbook

The major area of interest to you will be the review of over fifty blackjack systems. Also, this is the only book I know of that contains a complete bibliography of all the blackjack literature. *Blackjack: A Winner's Handbook* is available in most book stores or write for ordering information.

Personal Consultation

I offer a limited amount of personal consultation to advanced blackjack players. In an hour or two I can help you increase your card-counting speed, select an optimal betting table geared to your profit objectives and bankroll size, and show you some memory tricks for broadening your range of basic-strategy index numbers. This consultation is limited to players using the High-Low Point-Count System. As my time is expensive, I recommend that you investigate the BLACKJACK CLINIC and AD-VANCED BLACKJACK CLINIC before considering personal consultation.

Blackjack Bulletin

This blackjack newsletter is distributed only to graduates of my BLACKJACK CLINIC. I use it to keep all my students and former students up to date on course enhancements, blackjack profit opportunities from around the world and blackjack intelligence data (where the heat is and how to avoid getting barred).

CHAPTER 24

OTHER RECOMMENDED SOURCES of CASINO GAMING SERVICES

BOOKS

There is a multitude of books available on blackjack—twenty-five that I know of. The neophyte blackjack player is presented with a mass of confusion as he attempts to select those that will help him improve his game.

If you are interested in pursuing your study of blackjack, here are the books in addition to my book—*Blackjack: A Winner's Handbook*—that I recommend you purchase (listed in alphabetical order).

Beat the Dealer by Edward O. Thorp. New York: Vintage Books, 1962, 1966. This book originated the theory of card counting and is a must for all serious blackjack players.

Blackjack Super/Gold by Lance Humble with sections by Julian H. Braun. Las Vegas: B&G Publishing, 1979. This is a good book for beginners, with a lot of practical advice about blackjack.

Million Dollar Blackjack by Ken Uston. Hollywood, CA: SRS Enterprises, 1981. This is an outstanding book. It contains a complete description of the Uston Point-Count System, fascinating stories about Ken's team-play adventures and other interesting data about the world of blackjack.

Playing Blackjack as a Business by Lawrence Revere. Secaucus, NJ: Lyle Stuart, 1975. Another good book for the beginning blackjack player.

Professional Blackjack by Stanford Wong. La Jolla, CA: Pi Yee Press, 1980. This is a technical book, but it is a must for the serious blackjack player. It contains a thorough description of the High-Low System and, for the advanced player, tables of basic-strategy variations for varying casino blackjack rules.

MAGAZINES

Gambling Times. Gambling Times is the oldest surviving gaming magazine and consistently publishes interesting articles on all the casino games with an emphasis on blackjack. For subscription information write:

Gambling Times
1018 N. Cole Ave.
Hollywood, CA 90038

NEWSLETTERS

The following are my recommended newsletters for the serious student of the game.

Stanford Wong's *Blackjack Newsletters*. I think very highly of these newsletters. They are an excellent value for both the professional and occasional player. The newsletters contain tips on blackjack, answer reader questions, report liberal blackjack rules in casinos around the world, publish fascinating letters from blackjack professionals from world-wide locations and evaluate and compare various point-count systems. Write to Wong at Pi Yee Press, Box 1144, Dept. J, La Jolla, CA 92038 for information.

Casino & Sports. *Casino & Sports* is available from the Gambler's Book Club and contains many articles of interest to blackjack players. They publish about six issues per year. They are well worth the money and I recommend that all readers purchase a subscription. Write to:

Gambler's Book Club
630 So. 11th St.
Las Vegas, NV 89106

Rouge et Noir News. This is a newsletter devoted to the world of casino gaming. It contains many excellent articles on blackjack from a number of different perspectives: blackjack systems and book evaluations; card counters and their legal problems with getting barred (especially in Atlantic City); casino win rates, policies, and procedures. The newsletter also covers the industry at large by providing perspectives on casino management and focusing on casino problems. The newsletter is providing excellent coverage of the developing Atlantic City casino industry.

Readers who wish to stay abreast of the industry should consider subscribing to this publication.

For further information or for your subscription, write to:

Rouge et Noir, Inc.
PO Box 6
Glen Head, NY 11545

CASINO GAMING EQUIPMENT AND SUPPLIES

For the casino gamer interested in setting up his or her own practice and play facilities at home or at the club, there is an excellent source of gaming supplies and equipment available in the Philadelphia/South Jersey area—*Gil's Guide to Casino Gaming*.

Gil offers handsome, sturdy and fold-up blackjack tables for a low discount price—$375. Comparable tables run well over $500. You may even order the table with the Atlantic City basic strategy imprinted on the layout.

Gil also offers dealer's shoes, casino-like chips, discard holders, blackjack layouts and many other fine products, all at discount prices. Write directly to Gil for a catalogue:

Gilbert E. Stead
Gil's Guide to Casino Gaming
Dept. QP
1601 Fairhill Place
Clementon, NJ 08021
(609) 228-7277

About the Author

Jerry L. Patterson is a syndicated casino gaming columnist and the author of the popular *Blackjack: A Winner's Handbook.* His casino gaming column has been published in the *New York Daily News,* the *San Francisco Chronicle,* the *Philadelphia Inquirer,* the *Baltimore Sun,* the *South Jersey Courier Post,* the *Atlantic City Press,* and many other newspapers.

Mr. Patterson is an instructor of winning blackjack methods and founder and operator of THE BLACKJACK CLINIC—a blackjack school that has instructed over three thousand students in Blackjack's Winning Formula in the first three years of operation. He is an active professional blackjack player, playing and winning in casinos all over the world.

His background as a computer scientist serves him well

in the world of professional blackjack. Mr. Patterson developed a blackjack computer model with Will Cantey— one of the four developers of the original basic strategy.

Mr. Patterson enjoys giving practical advice to the occasional gambler. He has appeared on over fifty radio and TV talk shows.

Information Request Form

1. THE BLACKJACK CLINIC
   Please send a brochure
   including pricing information
   and a schedule of classes for:

   Phila./South Jersey   ☐
   New York   ☐
   California   ☐
   Florida   ☐
   Other _____ ☐
          please specify city

2. THE ADVANCED
   BLACKJACK CLINIC
   Please send pricing
   information and a schedule of
   classes.   ☐

3. BLACKJACK
   CORRESPONDENCE
   COURSE
   Please send me information.
                          ☐

243

4. BLACKJACK CLINIC
   FRANCHISE
   Please send information on
   how I may establish a
   BLACKJACK CLINIC
   franchise.   ☐

5. CASINO GAMES CLINIC
   Please send information
   including pricing and a
   schedule of classes.   ☐

6. MICROCOMPUTER/
   ASSISTED BLACKJACK
   TUTOR
   Please send me information.
   I do/do not (circle one) own a
   personal computer.   ☐

Please call at any time for further
information (609) 772-2721 (N.J.
Residents) or Toll Free (800)
257-7130.

NAME_____

Street
Address_____

City/State/Zip_____

Phone_____

**SEND TO: Jerry L. Patterson
Casino Gaming Specialists
One Britton Place, Dept. WF-2
Voorhees, NJ 08043**